HEALING OUT LOUD

HEALING OUT LOUD

Finding Your Voice
Through Painful Growth

Yaritza Ruiz

Dedication:

This book is dedicated to everyone who helped me through the darkest time of my life thus far, thank you for holding me on the days I felt weak and confused, and for listening when all I had was pain.

To my children, you are the reason I fight to heal. I am doing the work now, so you don't have to.

This is for the people who know the ache of family silence and may need some tools. It is not normal. It is toxic. You are not alone.

And to every soul suffering in silence, holding on to family for the sake of love and unity, even when it breaks you inside, this is for you.

"Live your truth. It fuels your soul."
~Yaritza Ruiz

Table of Contents

Introduction

This is truly a story of the effects that occur when we place virtual reality lenses on fuckery. I always thought that if I wrote a book it would be about being a teen mom, the journey, the struggle, and the perseverance. My story would include the trauma of being sexually abused and the continued chosen oblivion surrounding it. Or maybe a combo book with my husband about being in a relationship since our teenage years, growing from infidelity and emotional immaturity to a successful marriage.

This is not the most scandalous story in my life but definitely the darkest one I've had to grow from. I am sharing a story of generational fuckery. We hear a lot about overcoming it, addressing it and overall breaking it. Yet, no one talks about how it feels to actually burn that familial bridge, to make a declaration for yourself and your future.

I thought by 2019 that I had gone through all the work needed, therapy and all. I loved my family as they are. I struggled knowing core values were different, yet it was always family above all else. Messy, chismoso, loving family. But in 2022, one text message changed everything I thought. My entire family dynamic changed in an instant, with one decision, passed through the "family" gossip chain. Everything stopped. The calls, the gatherings, the BBQ's, Sunday dinners on Football Sunday, birthday parties - all of it! It felt like death. The death of (fill in the blank). I felt defeated. The cumulative agreement that I was wrong made me feel weak. I had used a mantra for a long time, "Don't make sense of shit that makes no sense," but in this case I found it hard to apply. None of these actions and choices made sense. How can so many people go along with a lie?

It became painfully clear that no matter how much I tried it made no impact. Ultimately, I was to be silenced. I began to understand that it wasn't my place to correct the narrative or to demand honesty. This was to be a part of my story, and I had to embrace it because I was on the verge of an emotional breakdown, and some days I did break down. I started praying for my confusion to be converted into peace and for the ability to accept something I did not understand. Despite the bloodline we shared, I was not privy of all the details of family matters. It took me a while to realize that if you were not a part of the toxicity, you were a part of the problem. Silence, complacency and neutrality are all the enabling tools of toxic family dynamics.

In New York, after the terrorist attacks, we would commonly hear the phrase, "See something, say something." It is our duty, as Americans, to say something if we see something. Yet, in other spaces, we can choose to be blind to certain things. Isn't that ironic? As humans, we seem to pick and choose what should get our reaction. We choose what is blasphemous and inappropriate. I naively had expectations that certain people would have my back, defend me in rooms I was not in, and address me directly with any narrative brought to them.

So many years of fighting. Fighting for acceptance and fairness. Shouting about being molested, double standards, mistreatment, and the support of fuckery. But the response was either silence, dismissal or downplay. Through the years there were a few people who encouraged me to continue to be me. They encouraged me to be vocal and change the course of the world I want for my future, my kids, their kids, and their kids' kids. Now I choose to heal out loud.

I have always struggled with staying quiet about something that bothered me. I found myself losing sleep, wrestling with dreams or being emotionally consumed when something just seemed off to me. There is a human need for consistency. We all know consistency helps our health and our physical fitness but what about the consistency in fighting fuckery? What does that help? Do we not stay in that fight? Fighting to spread the word of things that are unacceptable. To encourage taking action behind those prayers instead of just praying?

What I needed was an affirmative declaration that the events of my life did not make me a victim. If anything, these events have empowered me. All of the stories I've lived through have brought me here to share this with you. I have been trusted to experience these human events in order to help those around me and those coming after me to learn from their trauma. To maintain gratitude through the hurt and pain. To analyze things from this perspective: "What is God trying to tell me or show me?" Rather than asking, "Why is this happening to me?"

My hope is that those who read this are the ones who strive to be a better person every day because every day is not the same and we are not perfect. We are learning every day with every interaction and retention of information. Are you that person?! Awesome, because if not, you are still welcomed to be nosey, my life is pretty dope and if you are looking for a sign that God is working His magic at His pace, I am it! In the words of Lizzo, "If you're looking for a sign, bitch, I'm it!" No, but for real, remembering 1 Corinthians 10:13, which assures us that God will never give more than you can handle, this kept me above water. And hopefully it does the same for you as you make the choice to heal out loud, too.

Chapter 1
It Ends With Me

"I heal as I reveal," Kirk Franklin

"Forgive them father for they know not what they do."
Famously in the Bible but also from Lauryn Hill's
***Miseducation* album.**

B elieve it or not, the catalyst of this story is a simple text message. How did we get to this text message? How could a text message change everything? Have you ever experienced the abrupt end of a relationship with minimal explanation? It is not easy to make sense of the dissolution when there is not a clear moment to pinpoint the deceleration. It took this one text message and the domino effect of that choice to catapult me into mourning the closest relationships I had. It took the shift of how I was treated for me to realize the narcissistic behavior that fueled narratives which consequently led to my life changing in ways I was not ready for.

At this point, I had been listening to Ed Mylett for a few months, and he said, "You're the one." You're the one to make the change. His podcasts changed my life and way of thinking. Full disclosure, you may get tired of hearing about Ed, but he's my guy. He helps me "max out" my life and reminds me that I'm meant to do something great.

Little did I know a prayer I began reciting in 2021 and the beginning of 2022 to "remove those from my life that no longer serve me or my future," meant removing almost everyone who was a part of my life. Be careful what you wish for. It led to many days in which I was unable to celebrate the good things happening in my life. I cried a lot.

Where were my cousins and aunts? Why didn't my parents ask me any questions, why didn't my best friend confirm stories about me? When it became clear that the narrative about me was accepted rather than questioned or defended, I questioned the relationships I held dear. It was clear that there was no need to explain myself. Confusion filled my heart and mind. Even as I write this I still struggle with some confusing emotions.

The morning of Noche Buena (Christmas Eve, a sacred and highly celebrated day in the Puerto Rican community), I woke up with huge imaginary bricks on my chest. The pressure, likely heartache, birthed the declaration that I did not deserve this treatment from my family. Distance would speak louder than words. I no longer cared to be a part of their family or the lies that fueled the fuckery. This was the beginning of a mourning period for each person. The expectations I held of their presence in my life faded as the reality of my new world became clearer. I had no choice but to move on. I had made my announcement to the matriarch in my world at that time, my mother. News got around. No one else rang my line. My existence and presence was already not needed or expected for six months and that morning, I was ready to step into the painful truth and find my voice.

Up until the morning of Christmas Eve in 2022, I felt like a child on punishment, waiting for my parents to be okay with me. Then, it hit me like a ton of bricks, "I don't deserve this." Up until then, I had wondered what the narrative was that warranted the exile of my husband, my children and me from the family. It almost felt like I was standing up for myself in an abusive relationship. The bricks on my chest were so heavy, I knew I had to make a change for my future. I knew this would not end. Don't get me wrong, it is not easy to stop the emotional part of the brain from spiraling at times. I caught myself plenty of times asking, "What did I do?", "How can they treat me like this?" or "Why, why, why?"

This way of thinking does nothing but beat you up. There are no logical answers to those questions. Can we apply grace without excusing the behavior and choices of others? Yes. Yet, at times this feels like it does nothing for you, your healing, or your growth. The former doesn't increase the path of your purpose, or does it? We have to ask ourselves, 'What is the lesson I need to learn?' We are here to learn lessons. We are here to make the world a better place. Ed says, "We are here to do something great."

My declaration, "I don't deserve this", was sent via a text to my mother. It felt like a relief because the text message and everyone's response or lack thereof had been consuming me. I was doing my best to have conversations with my parents, but it was not working. I couldn't continue to play the "we don't talk about Bruno" game. Communication with my parents had to completely end. I felt forced to make the decision to accept that I was cut off by my family. Otherwise, I could not allow myself to enjoy my time with my husband, children and those that wanted to be around me. All my moments were overshadowed with the pain. I found myself wrapped up in self-pity. So, I HAD to choose me. Ed says, "You have to work through the pain." Not understanding why I was exiled, compiled with anger and sadness, I was in full mourning mode. Mourning those who are alive is gut wrenching. It's really mourning the life, the relationship, the future you envisioned. But there was no choice. I had to be silent toward them rather than continue a life of silence with them. Slowly, family members transitioned to "relatives" and those who were considered family have reduced significantly.

In a podcast interview on The Ed Mylett Show, Jaime Lima said, "People stopped seeing my light, my value." And maybe that's it. It sucks that part of the story includes the burning of bridges and dissolution of decades of friendships and lifetime relationships. It is not an easy decision, which is a big reason why I'm sharing chapters of my life story now. For years, I found myself doing things to be a part of or be considered a friend or loyal to family members. Yet, I was struggling to converse and filter more than I used to. I was having physiological responses like nausea and heart pain when I did. I don't question God's work, though. I believe this is a part of the growth. As confusing, sad, different, lonely and fucked up as it may be, I am riding it out. I don't know what it's prepping me for, but I know overall the mentality, reality, and the treatment of me and mine required a sever and re-evaluation of what the fuck we were doing here.

However, this was not my first attempt at setting boundaries. I experienced re-traumatization in 2018 which I will get into a little bit more later on. At that point in my life, I chose to lead with gratitude in order to remain close to my family. The feeling ballooned in me. I was so grateful to have a mother, a family, longevity, unity, customs and traditions. As long as I played along, I was good in all familial relationships. I was a pleaser. This time would be different. My decision to accept the estrangement in its truest form meant I stopped tolerating, pleasing, or accepting the fuckery. I stopped silencing myself, the painful truth showed itself. It became my power instead of my muzzle.

I needed to figure out how to use my pain as an example and refrain from being a dagger of emotions. I feel like a part of my purpose in life is to learn and share. It is to follow my passion and make an impact on those around me. Like Ed Mylett says, "We are best equipped to help the person we were." To know who you are, you must brace yourself for the painful shedding of the parts of you that you've held within your identity. So, for me, my pain slowly became my power.

I hope sharing my pain and the journey can help you ease yours. This happened for me, not to me and it is not about me. It is about the human who has gone through this, doesn't know how to go through it, or will go through it at some point in their lives.

Chapter 2
Chrysalis

No matter what, I'll love you endlessly
But I gotta run, I gotta run from your reality
I know we're blood, but this love is bad for me
"Bad for me" - Meghan Trainor (ft. Teddy Swims)

Family is a concept that seems to be redefined for me as time goes by. It is typically defined by the labels placed in your blood lineage. Having my first daughter at fifteen, I knew I wanted to keep a strong family dynamic around her. Afterall, some of my fondest memories involve family gatherings. They are so precious to me. The moments with my aunts, uncles, and cousins. The crew got smaller as we got older, but the energy was always the same. These events were filled with good food, music and dominos. This is something I always appreciated, and I wanted to replicate all the things I loved as a kid. You become who you know to be, and I had amazing examples.

The decision to separate yourself from your family, your traditions, and your normalcy is not something typically impulsive or irrational. It involves a series of events. An accumulation of fuckery so to speak. You will have signs. You will feel it coming but that does not mean you will be ready for it. It's so easy to see clearly in hindsight and understand how all those cues were warnings. I was in the compromise phase with my parents. Wanting to hold on to them but knowing it meant rewriting history, changing what I knew to be true and ultimately, going along with actions and accepting what did not sit well with my values and the values I want to instill in my children. Have you ever had someone in your life that you knew should not be granted access to you, but you still found ways to keep communicating to hold on to the parts of them you love? Gratitude was the foundation of the negotiation I was doing in my mind and heart. As you get out of a relationship it's natural to try and negotiate terms, so you don't fully lose the person.

Yet the terms in this instance mandated rewriting history. I had to go along with ignoring the existence of a family member, continue to be silent about a pedophile, accepting generational dysfunction and selective outrage. It happens too often. Families that protect a pedophile, so they look good to the outside world. I would often put it in present terms: if one of my brothers molested my kid, would it be okay? I began to question the character of all my family members. From the ones who refused to ask the right questions to those who blatantly pacified offenses. Who encourages their pedophile brother to stay away from little kids rather than get them help? Who won't protect their children and mental health over secrecy and fuckery? I often went into spirals of questions that left me feeling alone, angry, and misunderstood. It took severed ties and reduced access to me for the spiraling of my why's and what the fuck's to stop.

This reminds me of reality TV crime shows, and how there is almost always someone who says, "They would never;" or "I could never imagine they would do that." This whole ordeal and similar traumatic events can cause you to feel like you truly never knew someone and/or their thoughts. Yet the labels that were placed on me, I took seriously. Sister, godmother, daughter, and cousin; these labels became a part of my identity. My role as a big sister was important to me.

To be in my life means I will push you, challenge you, and expect you to be held accountable for your choices. However, this was not seen as acceptable nor helpful, instead it was received as disloyal and difficult. The list of things that did not sit well with my values and the values I want to instill in my children grew longer and became heavier. The consistent failure to hold family members accountable and ask questions or apply pressure to demand truthfulness was already percolating inside me. Yet, as a daughter and sister, my loyalty was required. A loyalty that was placed on me through unspoken expectations. Pressure to "be family" was applied.

You've heard the story a hundred times, in a hundred different variations. A family chooses to stay quiet or act as if things did not happen. The standard, "We don't talk about what happens in this house." As young kids, we look up to our parents even if we don't realize we are doing it. We are taking in our nature to figure out our place and role in this world. We were proud Puerto Ricans who enjoyed our culture through food and music. We were loud, domino playing, family-loving people. We were clean and maintained a clean house.

My upbringing definitely gave me great functional human skills. The one consistent thing was that the past was rarely discussed unless it was surrounded by gossip or a funny memory. I never once thought, until my own re-traumatization, that my mother had failed to do the work to heal her own traumas. Never realizing that this led to the creation of a life adjusting to traumas rather than confronting them and healing from them. Remaining a strong independent woman was the focus. I wanted to understand her story, and how she silently accepted things.

Yet I could no longer go along with what was considered normal when in fact, it was toxic. You may be able to relate to this when it comes to friendship. Have you ever spent time with a friend and left feeling like you outgrew them? It happens over the course of time. The conversations start to feel more euphoric than progressive. As I got older and started partaking in conversations with the adults I started to understand the way they think. A slow accumulation of selective memories, selective moral application and standards, the recreation of history and acceptance of "family" was not something that I could continue to be part of despite how amazing and familiar those good times felt.

Choosing to be blind to some things yet make an uproar about others baffled me. Choices. It quickly became clear that some are respected in the "family" just not everyone. The criteria for what classifies as acceptable was not consistent. This became a major source of my frustrations and confusion and slowly crippled my thinking. As humans, we expect others to act or respond as we would but that just leads to heartbreak. We are unique. Sometimes, it is hard to remember that. You and I can look at the same thing and see two totally different things. It is not easy to break this expectation because it is masked by the shock of audacity. Have you ever asked yourself, "How can they do that?" This is where audacity breeds. Comparing how I would react "if this or that happened to me" does not help. Rather, I have begun to ease my confusion and pain by reminding myself that this is their story too. The decisions a person makes does not reflect on me. It is how they want their story to play out.

That didn't stop the yearning desire to be heard and understood, but the pain and realization that I deserved more was bigger. Now it wasn't just about me, it was about my kids, my future, my mental health, my legacy and my integrity. I spent the first six months of this period crying a lot, not allowing myself to appreciate and be grateful for the blessings I did have. I was growing a business, going from a home office to a rental office with Chamber of Commerce recognition; yet I could not allow myself to be happy about these accomplishments. I was doing to myself exactly what others had done to me as a teen mother. Instead of giving myself kudos for what I was accomplishing, I constantly reminded myself that I no longer had a relationship with so many people I loved.

Waking up every morning and living with that decision was a different monster to battle. I was not prepared for it. All I knew was that I could not go on knowing that the way I experienced certain events was being convoluted with falsehood. What's worse, I shared blood with and held great love for the partakers and neutralists. Fuckery was overseen because of bloodlines and unspoken loyalty. I was told I was making a mistake. I reflected hard and could not quite pinpoint it. Why was I so passionate about this? Why did I care so much about this situation? My answer was that I saw myself in other little girls - in my daughters and my nieces. I wanted to be vocal for them but more for the little girl in me who was too scared before. I embraced my black sheep status by listening to Taylor Swift's new song *Anti-Hero*, "I'm the problem, it's me."

The thoughts ran like a rollercoaster, from how all of my family members' connections would only deepen with unified God praising and sharing events after the text to the mutual dislike for me and dismissal of my husband and kids. While silent partakers and enablers, like my aunts, cousins and even close friends played along, the pain increased with every passing day. You truly must "go through it to get to the other side." I cannot quite say "get over it" because the pain is not something you get over, but you get used to it, make peace with it, and even accept it. This is how we change and avoid becoming and duplicating what we've seen. Every day I want to be better. Better than what I saw. Better than how I was treated.

We're all messed up in some way, which is why we should just be kind. No one knows what another person is going through, has survived, or is surviving.

Most importantly, we have to be kind to ourselves. Are you listening to your intuition? Are your boundaries stronger than your empathy? Have you allowed yourself to process? The hardest part is realizing there is a lesson to be learned from your painful experience. In addition to feeling the pain of mourning relationships I thought I'd always have, I had to sit in the pain and allow its magic to work. Napoleon Hill said, "If we survive the temporary pain, we will meet the other version of ourselves."

In the thick of the pain I read the book, *Forgiving What You Can't Forget*, where Lysa Terkeurst said, "We have to get to a place where the pain we've experienced is a gateway leading toward growing, learning, discovering and eventually helping others." Take a minute to think about anything that you have learned to do. Everything from feeding yourself or tying your shoes to learning a new profession or tool. There is a "hard" portion to the learning. When the pain is hard and fresh, it is hard to see its purpose. There were lessons I needed to learn and how I responded would determine how I handled it. The time it takes to learn the lessons, find the internal solutions and begin the healing is under your control.

I think of Ne-Yo's "Caterpillar" intro on his "Good Man" Album. "If you relieve the pain a caterpillar experiences while exiting the cocoon they will die. We must feel pain." I asked myself every morning for over a year, "Are you okay with this?" The answer always leaned on the severance being so much more of what I had to do versus what I wanted to do. I still held expectations for those who had wronged me. I expected an apology call, a check in, some fuck given! Why though?! These people are praying to have their lies and actions justified. They support one another. I felt freer but it hardly diminished the pain associated with my reality. I had to accept that living my truth challenged their fabricated reality. When the people you love start to make you feel like you're crazy, you have to get out. I felt trapped, consistently gaslighted and played. I had been silenced too many times.

Expectations truly become the death of most relationships. All of the expectations I held for my family members and friends have hurt me more than their actions. We, as empathic humans, hold people to standards and expect things from them that they would not expect from themselves. Expecting others to think as we do or treat us the way we would treat them is a set up. It is a set up for disappointment because we are all imperfectly human. With relatives, it was the expectation to care and be concerned enough to contact me and want to know why there is turmoil and distance. I expected invites to the family gatherings because the comfort and feelings of one member did not outweigh the love and unity of the entirety. Particularly with my mother, I expected her to validate me the way I validate my children, to express empathy and understanding for me, the way I would with my children. I also expected her to have certain conversations with me and not her niece or her sister. Why did they know the reasons behind my brother's decision, and I did not?

Lack of communication fuels toxicity. I always credit my psychology background for allowing me to appreciate the power of talking and expressing ourselves so we can heal and grow. The lack of coming back to the table and addressing the issues has failed the family I grew up with. They rely on the misconception that things will work out without action. A disillusion that solely prayer will make it right.

To be honest, I would like clarity and accountability. However, that is not what the herd decided. The decision to ignore without addressing the issues was solidified. Consequently, familial lineage and labels require us to support blindly and silently. We are expected not to question anything but to reaffirm it instead by sharing with others who do not know enough to question. As humans, we can create our own reality which is dangerous if it's unchecked. And if we find enough people who love us and our made-up narrative, we will be at peace. But it is a false sense of peace. It is keeping yourself in the bubble of what you want to believe. Perhaps accepting the reality that someone close to you has been malicious, hurtful, dismissive or even criminal will hurt too much. So you refuse to see that part of them, never acknowledging that the villain in one story may also be the hero in another.

Have you ever noticed that, as you grow in different aspects of your life, those around you begin to change? Finding peace in their exit and understanding that I don't have to control the narrative or their perception of me has been huge for my healing process. It is not easy, and every so often I feel sad knowing that life changes when you decide to no longer be silenced. This time was different though. Maybe because this was the second time, therefore I was more adamant about what I would not be a part of. The consistent practice of sweeping things under the rug was going to end with me. The expectations to move on and get over it was not acceptable to me. We must address so we can heal. The mama bear in me was ready to fight and knock down doors after seeing the hurt in my babies' eyes when they said, "We haven't seen our uncle in a long time;" or "I didn't know what to say when Abuela called me, it's been a long time since we spoke." They went from seeing these relatives twice a month to once a year and then not at all. The pain I was holding was not just mine, it was my kids' pain as well.

At times, I felt like I was going crazy, telling myself things like, 'Everyone disappoints you at some point,' or 'If I loved them, they'd eventually disrespect, disappoint, or betray me." It was a rough road to shift my mindset to believe these experiences did not make me a victim, they made me stronger and more cautious. One of the biggest hurdles I had to overcome was accepting that those I have put on a pedestal, whom I loved the majority of my life, and who I considered part of my "forever village" had failed me. These people individually and collectively failed to reciprocate the love and care I give. If I were to explain the depth of my family tree, it would amaze most people to know only one person reached out to me.

Only one blood relative cared enough to ask me questions and check on my mental health. These alleged God-fearing, church-going folk united as Judas in my world. They condemned me rather than comforted me. Although it has eased over time, emotional moments occasionally rise up like acid reflux.

It's a big emotional progression from the days in my youth when I leaned on Eminem's lyrics as an angry person. Now I'm trying to control my responses and heal without raging. All of this is going to help someone, this is going to strengthen a young person who feels misunderstood. For those "wrong in all the right ways" like Pink says. One day, there will be a person, young or old, who will see themselves in my story, in my human experience. I will remind them or empower them to stand up for the right to combat fuckery. It's not fun but dammit, it is necessary. How else do things change the world? The ones that stood up, took risks, and said, "This shit ends with me," they're the ones who changed the world. If it means less fuckery in the world then it's worth it. If it means living my truth and being real to me and my kids for their future and their kids' futures, then so be it.

Chapter 3
Change

But now I know things change for better or worse
You could say that I'm the same but
I adjusted to all the hurt
You can't promise me it'll be the same
'Cause sometimes change
Sometimes, sometimes change
"Sometimes" - H.E.R.

It was the most amazing BBQ my hubby and I hosted. Filled with family, friends, and the best Puerto Rican food a barbeque can have. Music played, drinks flowed, and we sang happy birthday to my dad. It was epic. Suddenly, everything changed so quickly and unexpectedly with just one text message. No one ever called me to ask me anything after that text message. What did I say to my brother? What did he say to me? No. Rather a story was told, and decisions were made at my expense. Now I was expected to simply accept it as a repercussion for my lack of loyalty.

"I prayed for peace in this decision and I'm at peace with it. I want to be direct so both of us can move on. I no longer want a relationship with you. I don't want you in my life in any kind of way. I harbor no anger or ill

**will towards you. I wish you nothing
but success and happiness. You'll
never hear from me again in this
lifetime and you'll only see me when
we're forced to bury those we love. I
don't want a response to this and any
response will be unread, no matter
where it comes from."**

I woke up to this text message two days after the BBQ. I immediately sent a screenshot to my parents, and their response was not expected. They were upset with me! My dad told me I should have minded my business, and my mother stopped talking to me altogether. There were no questions asked, no benefit of the doubt. No curiosity for clarity. It wasn't a surprise to them apparently. They were right though, this didn't come out of nowhere. There is always a series of events. With my brother, there were a lot of events. And I adored him the whole way because he was my little brother.

You see, I was seven when my mom went into full blown labor in the middle of the night. It was my 1st grade picture day too! That captured detail along with how I felt that day is still so vivid. I remember feeling so happy that my little brother was coming. Such fond memories of us growing up. Naturally, I was careless with him as a big sister which resulted in funny memories of me dropping him or kicking him in the face. I was popped for these things, but the punishment didn't prevent those moments from becoming sibling memories we laughed about as adults. We were close, despite the age difference. As I began healing and accepting his decision to no longer have me in his life, I started to remember some pivotal moments. Moments we never talked about.

One night during our regular family gatherings filled with music, food, domino games, and kids running around, my godmother looked over to me and said, "You look just like your father." I was about 11 or 12 years old. I instantly looked at her wide-eyed and then looked over at my brother who was standing there, confused. I don't think he realized that we didn't have the same dad until that moment. This is the moment that helped me realize children do not see color. Racism is taught. Up until that moment, when he was 4 or 5, he did not see that my skin was much lighter than his and our parents. I don't know how this affected him because he posed his questions to our mom. My questions afterwards were a little different. I asked my mom about my biological father while she stood in the kitchen cooking. She said, "He is either dead or locked up." The recurring explanation. My brother never asked me about my biological father. Ever! Even after I started to piece together the story of how I came to be when we found my biological sister in 2016.

When my brother started school, my mom taught me how to iron. That was my responsibility, ironing the creases in his uniform pants so he could look adorable. I really enjoyed being responsible for getting his clothes ready for school. I was taking care of him and helping my mom at the same time. I was also responsible for picking him up from school and walking home with him. It was just him and me for a long time. We shared a room, and he always wanted my attention like your typical annoying little brother. We spent so much time together watching movies and shows like *Space Jam, Little Rascals* and *Animaniacs*.

I remember watching WWE wrestling together and I would warn him to hide when Undertaker came out. He was so scared of his entrance music that he would run behind the couch until the music ended. Then I would hug or hold him when it was over. He was a little jokester too. He would take my keys and hide them. I think it was his way of getting me in trouble but what are little siblings for, right? It became a running joke as we got older.

He was about seven years old when I met my husband. We would bribe my little brother and offer to buy wrestling toys to get some alone time. One time we were under the sheets, and he came over and asked, "What are you doing?" Embarrassed, we asked him to leave after I said, "Nothing" but he pulled the covers while yelling, "So why are you naked?" I was about 13 years old at the time. This moment, while funny now, is shocking to my adult parental brain for so many reasons. He knew that not outing my actions to mom meant he could get a toy. I am not sure how many times we followed through with the promise but not long after, that wasn't needed. I wouldn't be living at home for much longer.

The expectation in the culture was that sexual activity was enough to be given to the boy and his

36

family. Therefore, waiting for pregnancy was a different parental strategy. I knew my mother would not be okay because once she noticed I liked boys she repeatedly stated, "You get pregnant, you get out." No further instructions. This was a notch up from how she was raised. By the time my parents found out I was expecting my oldest daughter, I was already four months pregnant. So, "you're pregnant, get out" was the understood outcome. It saddens me to think of how my mother felt during this time. Now, as a mother, I hear the disappointment in her voice a little differently. It must have been hard knowing the little changes were not enough. How did my brother feel? From one day to the next he no longer had his roommate. His normality changed at nine years old. His life experienced just as many changes as mine had.

As adults, my brother and I would joke about how we grew up with different parents. Parenting by far is the hardest job in the world and healing your inner child, combined with adulthood traumas while in the process of raising sane, functional humans makes it even harder. Later, I understood that it was more about our parents being at a different time in their lives when they had him. I understand now, as a mother of three with big age gaps, that you are a different person as you age and raise children. We become different people, as we should.

Knowing this, the part that was still challenging for me was my increased awareness that core values started to differ from one child to the next. The differences in parenting became more and more apparent, and it wasn't all necessarily because of their life stages. When I asked my parents why there was a disparity, the explanations were usually gender role driven or because they expected more of me. Despite being a great academic student, every report card from kindergarten through eighth grade highlighted my lack of self-control and suggested my behavior "needs improvement". While my brother was a quiet student who did just enough and that was perfectly acceptable. That pressure made me want to do better though. While the difference sucked, it made me work harder.

One year, my parents went on vacation and asked me to check in on my brother, who was now a teenager. One afternoon, I got a call informing me that he had been caught shoplifting in Manhattan. I was floored! Mainly because he was given everything he wanted, materialistically. He lacked nothing. When I pressed him, he admitted he had been doing it for a while. I told him how disappointed I was and that I would tell our parents when they returned. I did not want them to be surprised when they got the bill in the mail for the merchandise per what the store employee told me.

As promised, I told them what happened, but they laughed and brushed it off. When the bill came in the mail, they paid it, never once holding him accountable or questioning his thoughts, actions, or decisions. He was asked, "How'd you get cáught?" Ironically, I was caught stealing too when I was about twelve years old. I went into the Edwards Supermarket on Broadway & 234th St. I walked around with my friend throwing things in the cart while my pager went off, calling attention to myself. As we tried to check out, we were pulled to the side for the things I put in the bag from the discount store I had stopped at first. My mother was called to pick me up. She yelled and beat me with an umbrella outside of the store, through the parking lot and halfway toward our building. The yelling continued followed by a lecture from my dad and punishment. What a difference. Oddly, I am grateful for some of the disciplinary choices my parents made with me. It made me tougher, respectful, implemented consistency, and gave me structure.

Shortly after, my brother met the girl who would become his future ex-wife. I remember how smitten he was, constantly bringing her around. She was sweet and I "big-sistered" them to death, always asking about birth control. One day he called to ask me for "help with morning sickness for a friend." I instantly knew but played along anyway. When the parents found out, she moved in. Now this was a major blow for me. I didn't quite understand. He was 18 and she was 16, and she was able to move in. To me, they accepted this because it was their son. I wondered, did they expect her to have an abortion? Tell her family?

Throughout her pregnancy, he and I bickered a lot. It was a lot of me being annoying and trying to hold him accountable and question his future plans. He addressed this by writing me a very long email two months before his first child was born. He said, "I just feel like you don't respect me for what I'm trying to build and what I'm trying to do because you've done it, and it hurts me so much." He was vulnerable with how I made him feel, expressing that when I treat him like a child "our bond suffers." He addressed watching me grow up, "I probably know more stuff about you than anyone, I've seen your tears, people hear about the ass kicking you got but I took them with you, I had to watch every single one of them and not be able to do anything."

We never really talked about what life was for him after I left. He once told me, "You left me with them." That statement did not impact me as much as it does now. I thought he had it easier than me. I chalked up every parenting discrepancy to him being their "Golden Child." The one they had together. I even bought him a shirt one Christmas that said, "Mom's Favorite". But I never processed what he may have experienced while growing up without me in the home. Maybe he expected me to protect him. In reflection, I realized we never talked about any of it. Not his dad being my stepdad, not the addictions, not his divorce, not family dynamics, the abuse or the fuckery. None of it. In his email, he reminded me, "I love you sis, and you need to realize that respect is a mutual thing."

His email also predicted the future, "I want our kids to be close…but if we are not strong, the future of our family looks dim." Signed, "I will always be here for you until my last breath, believe that, love your brother."

When I reread the email from 2009 after the text message I got in 2022, it was filled with subtle warnings. Warnings that I now understand were meant to set the foundation for his diminishing tolerance of

40

me. "The future of our family looks dim." I'm sure the first time I read it, these words did not stand out. Yet here we were fifteen plus years later understanding the power of words. The realization that he was keeping score of the times I hurt him. The times he felt disrespected or outdone by his older sister was enough for him.

We never discussed how my outspoken ways may have hurt him or how having a sisterhood type of relationship with his ex-wife years later made him feel. My tendency to play devil's advocate was frowned upon by my family. My parents bad mouthing his ex was not okay to me. They failed to see the effects postpartum and miserable energy brought around this young woman had on her. They failed to see her daddy issues bubbling over once she became a wife and mother. They didn't realize the pressure they were putting on her to be the perfect mother and wife at only 18. But I did. I did not see my brother as a sole victim because I too was in the middle of a shitty marriage, and it takes more than infidelity to break up a marriage. Where was the accountability for any possible contribution on his part? Why were these conversations putting the man on a pedestal? Apparently, I was the only one who felt this way.

Despite spending a lot of time together especially between 2010 and 2013, my brother and I never talked about any of it! Yet, during this time we became inseparable. We spent weekends together doing nothing or going out to bars with friends. He acted like a big brother most nights when I was drinking. I would drive to his house, clean, play music, lounge, and play with the kids. It was a season in which we talked a lot but now I realize we never had the necessary conversations.

Shortly after his first daughter was born, my brother and his wife moved to Connecticut. Thereafter, they moved into a bigger house in Bridgeport, and I loved it! I found myself going there often to escape from my own mess. Unfortunately, at this time, I was approaching what felt like the finish line of my marriage but didn't realize that my brother and his wife were at the end of the stretch for their union. I never knew to what extent, or the details that led to their divorce because that conversation never happened with either of them. What I knew was that this was a very traumatic time for him as he experienced being abandoned by his wife and left with their daughter.

While writing this book, my writing coach shared how she noticed that I displayed a shift in tone, energy, and even facial expression with just the mention of the word "brother". From that moment I started to put myself in his position and process the shit he may have experienced too. My parents responded very differently to helping him as a teen parent. Their help allowed him to finish training and schooling in order to get into the well-paid field he is in now. They took on the task of getting their granddaughter ready for school and all the things after school. Doing her hair and prepping meals, as needed. They pretty much raised her for two years. Then, he met the woman who would birth his second daughter. I'm not quite sure when, but that sure did solidify a consistent generational problem.

We learned that my brother may have fathered another child, and I remember being at my parents' place in the Bronx when the at-home test results email came in. He was pacing back and forth, super nervous. He entered his credentials and there it was, a positive result. This baby that he did not know, with a woman he slept with a handful of times, is his child. Still, we embraced it as a family. He would bring the baby around a couple times a month from the age of 7 months or so.

By that time, my marriage had made a turn for the better and I was pregnant with my youngest child. I fell in love with my new precious niece. Yet the presence of one person (a brand-new love in my brother's life) slowly changed the trajectory of having my new baby niece around. Within 6 months the fuckery became clearer. My brother's new person moved in with my parents, sharing a bed with my brother and his first daughter. I was baffled! If it was me with a new man and my daughter in the same bed, I would be accused of exposing my daughter to a pedophile. Yet the double standards made it okay for two grown adults to sleep in the same bed with a young girl. This new person stayed in the house, laid up all day. Actions which never would have been acceptable from me. Selective outrage. I share this because of the dichotomy between what is acceptable for the child with a penis and the child with a vagina. At this point they were blatant.

At first, I did not notice that my baby niece was coming around less because I was caught up in adjusting to life with three children. And then, one afternoon, my brother called me while at work frantically asking for advice because his new person had just scrolled through his whole social media account and discovered that he had another child. All my responses were questions. "What?!" "What do you mean?" "She didn't know?" "She's been staying at the house, hasn't she?" Ultimately, my advice was to be honest about the whole thing, still thoroughly confused as to HOW she did not know when my parents had pictures of her, not to mention the pictures on his social media and his tattoo of two cubs (his two daughters). I later started to piece together the chain of events that led to this. And now that she knew the truth, just like that my niece started to come around again.

By 2016, I began to ask questions as we started to see less of my niece, yet again. I was given vague answers until my mother disclosed that he was questioning the DNA test. My parents ran with it, but I questioned the reasoning. I texted him asking why he would not share how he felt about his daughter. He responded by accusing me of being angry about something completely different from the issue at hand. We now have a term for this, gaslighting. It wasn't until recently that I realized he had a tendency to shame my emotions and reactions.

I was confused and hurt. I became an emotional bullhorn as I bitched about my brother to family and friends. He stopped talking to me for a brief time before our Abuela died that same year and I apologized to him at her wake. Afterwards, I shifted the way I approached the situation. I refrained from talking negatively about my brother and asking questions about my niece or her whereabouts. At least, not to him or my parents or anyone that supported those choices. I chose to be silent about the topic. We fed into the same narrative portrayed by the movie Encanto. The "we don't talk about Bruno" situation had increased.

I'm sure my relationship with his ex-wife played a huge foundational part of his problem with me but the largest stemmed from my boisterous spews about my disappointment in him and his choices with his second daughter. My insistence on holding him accountable and asking him questions about things he would rather act like never happened. And of course my opinionated ways when it came to family and those close to us. I truly thought we would be in each other's lives forever. Insisting on making him my youngest child's godfather now feels like a dagger because I argued with my husband about it while pregnant. I held my brother in high regard. I knew the man he could be, and I credited his choices, that were clearly affecting me, to his lack of maturity.

How could you spend so much time with someone, adore them and not know them? And he didn't know me either. We never had those deep and vulnerable conversations. He never asked and I never shared. I never asked and he never shared. At a time when I thought we were close, I connected with this child, his child. I came to understand that despite how close I thought we were, I was not privy to how he really felt at the time or anytime thereafter. It wasn't until I allowed myself to accept that I, in fact, didn't know him and our love and respect was not mutual that I started to see it differently. At the core, he didn't know me as a stepchild. I didn't know him as a scorned man.

However, I refused to not hold him accountable. I was consumed, but who was I? His Judge? Yet here I was trying to explain to him and anyone who can influence him how these choices would affect the whole family. I was pissed and called him an "unfit father". I started to feel like I was riding the rollercoaster of my brother's choices. Choices that I realized only months after they were in full effect. I was disgusted and very vocal about the situation.

Whether we like to admit it or not, other people's choices affect us. Everything from divorce to politics. What's worse, despite how close you may think you are to someone, do you ever really know them? Do you expect them to run their choices by you? Years later, here I was on a ride of emotions feeling the repercussions of my brother's word choices for the text message and this 15-year-old email:

"I prayed..." This line triggers so much for me. Religious coverups, hypocrisy, forced faith and the misuse of God and prayer. Those words, so familiar to me as the exact ones used to cover up and excuse behavior that is actually the opposite of holy and glorious.

46

"... we are forced to bury those we love." These words annoyingly made me think of death a lot. Ironically, not my death but the death of literally everyone else in my life. I began mentally and emotionally preparing for long-distance relatives to die or play out unexpected deaths in my mind. This text shot me into instant mourning. As I broke down the painful choice of words, I realized that only a person who's never experienced the death of a loved one would speak such words.

Then I listened to a podcast with Ed Mylett and John Edward, the medium. They talked about the rarity of thinking about our own death. We hardly ever do. Now with the exposure to this conversation I, consciously, try to think of my death. It is hard because it forces you to plan, but it is a good thing. Prepare! One phrase I learned from my years of networking is, "failure to plan is a plan to fail." My mind shifted to what I want to be remembered for, what impact I want my life and my death to have. It was about me and my quality of life now. How can I use my life to help others?

"...for our kids to be close." This was a previous request of his, from his 2009 email. We all went to Virginia for a week, as a family, in the summer of 2018. Considering our daughters were only ten months apart and were spending so much time together, they bonded instantly. They became instant best cousins. We got the cutest picture of my parents with two of their kids and their grandkids enjoying a day at the water park. Precious. It was really a great vacation.

That event led to constant requests from my little one to see her cousin. I was so adamant about keeping in touch with my niece, but I did not know why. To others, it came off as if I was against my family's collective decision to support my brother. It wasn't until later that I identified that the source of my emotions stemmed from not knowing my biological father. As the youngest child in a blended dynamic, I could not understand why we found ourselves again at odds. Ultimately, my decision to maintain a relationship with my niece confirmed the prediction that "the future of our family looks dim."

Chapter 4
Just a Girl

We'll only end up hating the child we may be creating.
Love Child, never meant to be,
Love Child, by society,
Love Child, never meant to be,
Love Child, diff'rent from the rest.
"Love Child" - Diana Ross

Not sure if he knew leaving me behind
Would leave a part of my existence blind
Curious if time missed brought a tear to eyes that chose to miss
my growth in this world
Raised with so much bliss but his love was always missed
Maybe one day he'll bump into me and know it was me.
See in my eyes that I'm a product of a life he chose to put aside.
Yet here I am a show of how to rise and not let your past define.
Poem to my "Bio"

sn't it amazing how lyrics to songs can be so therapeutic? They relate, they feel true. They speak your pain into melody, they describe your life. Music has always been a safe place for me. I listen to music religiously. I make playlists. As you may have gathered by now, music is a big part of me, my everyday life and mental health. It is also a huge part of my happy memories. Coming from a musical and lyrical family, words mean a lot to us, which is pretty ironic that words were exactly what was missing in our home. I grew up in a house full of music. Eclectic! My dad made us pay attention to how the words string together, the bars dropped, the hidden messages. It instilled skills in my brother and me, learning to use words in amazing ways. Writing is a big part of us. My brother is a songwriter as well as a poet. I also have used writing as an outlet for my confusion and frustration.

At the end of 2019, I came to some realizations about my relationship with my brother. During this time I was finding ways to continue the relationships I wanted. I had to find a way to be okay knowing that maintaining these relationships meant being silenced in many ways. The reality was that my brother was tolerating me. By now, our interactions began to feel more forced. I knew it after a conversation with him about his youngest daughter. The answers were vague. Engrossed in emotions, I wrote a poem that December and titled it, "You don't even fuck with me." But I didn't give it to him, I just wrote and saved it.

Writing to a person but never sending it is pretty therapeutic. When the pain hit in real time, I had the words, 'oh that's right! He doesn't even fuck with me.' It helped me lower my expectations of our relationship over the next few years before he sent me the text message. Don't get me wrong, we were siblings. We were cordial and laughed together at times. However something changed deeply. Even after I wrote my poem I tried becoming his guiding light as his Title Agent when he purchased his first home. He left my business an amazing review on Google and sent me the most heartfelt text messages throughout the process thanking and appreciating me. We really bonded again, or so I thought. Remembering those times feels like salt in the wound caused by the text message. Blocking me and eliminating me and my children from his life fueled an anger in me that really stemmed from unexpressed hurt and expectation of sibling unity, connection and communication. We shared a mom, how can he just erase his existence from my children who have known him their whole lives?

The hurt got the best of me at the beginning of 2023. I sent him a sympathy card. It was my own petty and therapeutic way of acknowledging his dismissal in spite of his promise that any reply to the text would go unanswered. I had no words at the time of the notorious text but one day the utter pain hit me as I shopped for a sympathy card for my cousin-in-law and her siblings who were starting the year with the loss of their mother. The purple flowers on the card caught my eye first, our mom's favorite color. The butterfly was me. I have a butterfly tattoo, because it symbolizes necessary painful growth. The words "Sorry for the loss of your sister" all stood out. Inside I wrote, "F U You narcissistic POS" and I stapled the poem. I don't know if he ever got it, or who else saw it. Did it make me feel better? A little. It was the beginning of my closure, yet it was also wrong. I used my words as a dagger. It served no real purpose and made no impact, but it did feel like a release, an acknowledgment of his decision.

I walked in pain everyday after that text, but many people had no idea. I leaned on a handful of people. This reminds me of the times I easily shared my pain with everyone. It wasn't until Martha, my high school counselor, came into my life that I had a safe place for that hurt, emptiness, and abandonment. I consciously stopped sharing my story once I got to college. In hindsight, the story was easily shared because I needed healing. There were never any conversations about it. I was never told how unacceptable it was. Sharing was my way of getting help.

I met Martha a few months after returning to 10th grade with my 2-month-old baby. She was introduced as my counselor, specifically assigned to teen parents in the school. I trusted her right away and opened up about it all. Everything from my boyfriend (later to be my husband) my mother-in-law, my own mother, my sexual abuse - all of it! I struggled with being a teen mom, too. I put a lot of pressure on myself because I did not want to live the life I had forever, nor did I want to live like those I saw around me. I was determined not to depend on my parents or in-laws forever. These things drove me, but Martha began the path of true healing for me. I needed to find ways to get through this new challenge and trauma with those I now had around me. I used my words wisely and healed out loud as much as I could.

Dealing with this new hurt, there were unexpected effects of the text message. It wasn't just the close relationships but nearly a third of the people that attended the BBQ, exited my life. Now those relationships had been reduced to holidays and birthday text messages which would slowly disappear. My eldest daughter and I started to develop a relationship with my cousin's daughter. Such an amazing little girl who already expressed gratitude for having a strong woman like me around her. But all those relationships are gone. One decision had trickling effects and made it all the more harder to stand in my truth.

In "The Four Agreements" by Don Miguel Ruiz, he says, "The truth is like a scalpel. The truth is painful because it opens all the wounds which are covered by lies so that we can be healed." How certain events were handled laid a big foundation for those wounds. And the way they weren't handled really shaped a lot of my future. It affected my thinking, drove my anger, and prevented healing. Yet the text message my brother sent had nothing to do with any of that. The text actually tapped into a part of me I was just getting to know.

The girl who didn't know her biological father and didn't know her history. Decades of events continued to slap me every day that I woke up and I reminded myself this was my reality now. My increased understanding of cultural and tribal fuckery became clearer. As I write this, I'm still battling, baffled, confused, and at times emotionally crippled on this road. Sometimes it's hard to decipher how things played out when, the truth is, I grew up well. Both things can be true. I was provided with food, a roof, good hygiene, family and good foundations. I have always felt different or misunderstood but I had a pretty decent childhood filled with great memories.

My mother, the youngest girl of seven siblings, was born in Puerto Rico. I have memories of seeing her face light up as she shared about her time as a young woman living independently in The Bronx. She was proud of her ability to take care of herself. She dated, worked, and lived her best life. She was so proud to have her own place when I was born. Reflecting on the pieces of her early life I see her face, her smile, and appreciate how she instilled my desire to be independent. She had me at a young age, just shy of twenty-one. She brought me into a dynamic where she depended on family. They became her support system for childcare. She made the decisions she thought were best for her and her child.

She dismissed my biological father from my life because he struggled with substance dependency. My whole life she dismissed my bio's existence, later telling me, "The best thing I did was give you a dad." In reflection, my guess was those statements were rooted in her disappointment of how she reared me. At the time she spoke these words she had already written herself off as a crappy mom who did nothing good for her first born but to provide a father figure.

My mother must have struggled with that a lot – seeing him in me, knowing I was always asking questions and challenging the dynamics of things. I remember when she pulled the pictures out from under her mattress. She gave them to me, and I stared at them for hours. It gave me more information to use when I looked for him. Something always told me that he thought of me, too. I have such fond memories of my mother singing "Love Child" by Diana Ross, so passionately. The lyrics resonate a little differently now. I have great memories of her dancing in the kitchen or singing and cleaning. There are times when I am cleaning, salsa comes on and there I go sounding just like her. My laugh is like hers and sometimes my facial expressions and responses are all her. Those things made the estrangement from my mother the most painful.

Such a heartbreaking feeling. It has become more and more apparent that there are unhealed parts to her and refusing to see me is her way of protecting her heart. She didn't want to hear about all her fuck ups during an intimate conversation with a third party she didn't know. Rather, uninviting me to holiday traditions and family events, and allowing narratives placed with no communication and silence won. Relationships died. Avoidance amplified it. Prayer pacified it.

One day, after a disciplinary session mixed with being popped and lectured, I wrote down on a piece of paper, "He is not my father." I tried to move it before my dad saw it but as he walked back in to come at me again, he froze. I noticed it, but he didn't address it. He finished what he said and that was that. Two days later, I forgot to make my bed when I got home so, when he got home, he went off. I got spanked and when he was done he yelled, "Go get your father." I knew then that he had seen it. Immediately, I felt so bad that I cried and went to the kitchen with pictures of my bio they had saved for me. I cried as I burned them. Suddenly, he came into the kitchen and asked me what I was doing. I told him I never wanted him to feel like I didn't love him like a father.

I believe this was when he shared with me that my Bio had come to look for me once and he sent him away because he did not want me to be raised or affected by someone struggling with drug dependency. So I had to walk around with the name of someone I did not know. It was a decision made on my behalf that no one spoke to me about at any time. There were parts of me I would never understand because it was normal for a child to not know a biological parent.

I think this triggered the rage I felt toward my biological father for the next five years. I would go around calling him "the sperm donor" and refusing to allow anyone around me to refer to him as anything else. I even started telling people to let me know if they found him because he owed me a lot of child support money. Reflecting on this now, I laugh. Poor young me, so angry and misguided. Desperate for more information in order to piece together the parts of me I did not know. I was hurting and it was showing up as anger and dismissiveness. I'm hurt even knowing that this can and will be the story of many little girls, wondering why. Why did their father not come see them? How can they be so easily forgotten?

The topic of my Bio's existence came back up when I was 17. By now I was living with my boyfriend and his family on the other side of the Bronx. We wanted to get married, but we needed the permission of my biological parents since I was a minor. Our only option was to run a newspaper article for six months announcing our search for him which would have cost us money we didn't have. Only adding to my resentment. How can he have a say when he wasn't even around!? Little did I know he wouldn't have seen it anyway, since he was in Pennsylvania at the time. He died six months before I got married, two years later.

I was a love child. Lost child. Emancipated with restrictions from someone I did not know and about whom I had only heard shitty things. Yet that didn't ease the desire to know who he was. His story. I slowly started to feel like I just wanted to know my sister and not him. However, life happened, and it didn't come up again. Not until 2016 when my eldest child began to question my looks. This led me to ask my mother to tap into her memory and try to find my sister. It took her two days. I started to get so many answers about Bio. It is so nice to find my sister. My aunts all knew about me. They love me and I got to meet my grandmother before she passed. It was a true blessing to finally put parts of my story together.

I had a great father-figure, but it never stopped me from wondering. My mother started dating my dad when I was so young. I love the story of their beginning, when you eliminate the fuckery. She would take me to the local park, and he just so happened to work across the street. He saw her, she played hard to get waiting 3 months to even kiss him. He later said he saw her in his dreams years before they met. There are so many little fairytale parts in their love story. It really showed me that this kind of love can exist. They've adored one another at times, really had one another's back. By the time I was five, I was calling him "Papi Jay". He would teach me things, and I always felt safe with him. My dad became a very big part of my life.

After a few "reality TV" moments in their relationship, my dad seemed to settle down. They had a child together, my little brother of course. Our family became more stable. Dad was always around, it was the four of us. Mom, dad, lil' bro and me. My dad has children from before and during his time with my mother, before they married. I saw less and less of my stepbrother for a while. We were a blended family, it was magical at times. He was my dad and always made me feel like his daughter. Maybe that's why my mom considers him to be the best thing she ever did for me?

I learned a lot from my mom as well. I admired her. She took me almost everywhere before she had my brother. I was like her sidekick. I remember how pretty she was and the fun energy she had. When the time came to teach me about womanhood, she passed down what she thought was important. "Women don't cheat"; "You have to cook, clean, etc." Clean house and good hygiene. But there was so much more I learned from just watching her. Ed says, "Most things we learn are caught not taught." I watched her get us ready for school, make sure we ate, go to work and come home to cook a meal for her family every night. Rarely did we eat out or order food. I learned how to be a good host, a good friend, a believer in faith, how to enjoy music, and dance...a lot. I always say she's a great person. She really did the best she could with me.

I have worked hard not to blame her. After listening to a podcast episode with John Bishop and Ed Mylett, hearing how blame is carried in order to keep a past feeling. This made a lot of sense to me. John said, "We find ways to reaffirm who we are everyday." Doubling down on conclusions we have made in order to say, "You see," even if it is to ourselves. For example, have you ever scrolled on social media and found all the memes that apply to your life? Have you heard something about a person who hurt you in the past and thought, "Yup, you see!" This is what John meant and throughout the healing process you will find that happening often. One that stands out to me, yet I struggle to apply, was a clip from an Alicia Keys interview where she said, "You can't expect things from people that they are incapable of giving."

As I write this, I want to be clear that I love my mother. While it is expected for a child to outlive their mother, losing a mother is not something everyone is prepared for. I've witnessed a lot of loved ones lose their mothers. It only made me more grateful to have mine. I remember when my co-worker lost her mom. I felt so blessed to be able to call my mother just because I could. Often, I would say that out loud or as a response when she would say, "What's up?" "Nothing, just calling 'cause I can."

For someone who disagreed with her on core fundamentals, I kept my mother super close. I wanted her close! I thought we were best friends. I thought she was my biggest cheerleader. It increased my appreciation for all the times she was genuinely a loving mother towards me and all the things I caught in her attempts to teach me. My lack of appreciation for our differences may have contributed to the severed relationship. As amazing as someone can be, their core beliefs, opinions, and way of thinking are what attracts you to want them in your life more than not.

I've heard it is healthy to love someone who has a different opinion than you. I've learned to avoid certain topics with her, like men in her family, gender roles, and infidelity. We have very different opinions when it comes to those topics and more, yet I always chose to see the good.

Not feeling supported by my mother during certain moments influenced how I interacted with her. She didn't see my heart and why I made certain choices in my marriage. She did not understand why I did not condone my son being exposed to sex at thirteen. I wanted to educate and listen to my children. I wanted to be more transparent and real, apologize, and learn from my kids. Yet carrying my mother's blame and judgment was not going to allow me to heal or give her enough grace so she can heal.

The way I wanted to handle things was not well received. I asked her to go to therapy with me again.

She refused; and sharing the positivity, transformation and healing was not enough to convince her. I had to apply one of the four agreements here. As a human, a mother, and a woman, I can understand and empathize with the fact that she may never be ready to speak on things that hurt, things that may not be as important to her. It was not personal, going to therapy with me meant walking into a room full of mirrors riddled in my pain. I had to shift my desire to help her understand me. I spent some time questioning why she would not dedicate time to improving her relationship with me. Yet again, I was comparing her to what I would do for my kids. Reminding myself of Alicia's words. Let me stop setting my mom up to disappoint me.

The silence was suffocating. All the things I already thought I was healed from were coming back up. I had to be defiant once again, the renegade who was vocal at eleven about being molested. I would often tell my mother that I would kill her brother. At twenty-one, I told the majority of the family about the molestation after we buried my Abuelo in 2005. Or the re-traumatization and pain that thirty-three-year-old me endured when I realized that the toxic mentality of protecting and concealing continues. Lies. I spent years battling and I was exhausted.

Chapter 5
Brace Yourself

For I know the plans I have for you...
Jeremiah 29:11

I want you to know that, I am the man who
Fight for the right, not the wrong
Seeing this and Seeing that
Going here and going there
Soon you will find out the man I'm supposed to be
Bam Bam - Chaka Demus and Pliers

Identifying your triggers can blossom a new path of healing. We are all responsible for our triggers. We must identify them so we can learn to control them. Instinctively, however, we have learned to protect ourselves by reacting. We lash out and shut people out. Some people unfortunately take things to criminal levels because of an impulsive defensive mechanism. We feel a need for protection from that time (or cumulative times) in our lives when we felt pain, those triggers. In my case, the pain was being dismissed, disregarded and ignored by people I loved most.

Thankfully, one of my sisters became a big part of my healing process after the infamous text message. She encouraged me to keep my crown on and adjust it as often as needed. As I spoke with my sister one morning during our regular "church sessions", she said, "It's all a test. A test of your growth, your level of response and ability to control distractions sent to slow down the path to your destiny." Ed Mylett, I believe, said, "Your focus equals your feelings." I keep this phrase in my daily activities, consciously redirecting my focus to prevent my feelings from bringing me down and reducing my productivity. Doing this allows you to be present in what you are doing. It increases gratitude. Reminding myself of this has allowed me to enjoy my blessings and my progress.

Trust me, it is a conscious effort. The rage in my heart is real at moments. Sometimes I felt like I was winning but other times I felt like I had to remind myself that I was not a violent person. I would constantly reinforce that this is the consequence for refusing to be part of the fuckery mentality. Filtering and silencing myself was no longer an option. I will continue to heal and fulfill my purpose, telling myself, "Let them google me." This is the attitude I needed in order to keep my crown straight!

One of the last text messages my mother sent me before I went silent for almost two years was, "I will pray for God to rebuke all the evil." I was confused. Who or what was evil in this scenario? The following year, communication was limited to birthday texts and not much more. I had to tell myself, 'This is what they wanted and what was needed.' Although I had made the final decision to remove myself. I was unaware that the actions and decisions to exclude me had been in effect for almost six months. Instead of feeling like a victim, this time, I decided that I was going to be the matriarch in my world. I decided I would start new traditions and fill my future with what I wanted. As the main character in my story, I control what I am focused on. "Focus is your feelings" right? I was now focused on being a better mother and a healed daughter who is grateful rather than bitter. Intentionally working on me so that maybe, one day, I can speak to my parents without expectation of being seen, heard, and understood.

The estrangement from my family ignited a reflection of my life. I had an epiphany, realizing my memories and recollection of things were just that, mine. The other thing I learned in psychology is that we live a subjective life. We are the main characters in our own world. Even those who live for others, do for others, and are considered selfless, are also the main characters in their worlds. Because we are the main characters, we tend to associate things, smells, and feelings with experiences we have had. We're all conditioned by our experiences and that's what makes us so unique. This is why we can have a shared experience, be raised by the same parents, and still have very different outlooks on the same events.

While the shock never ceased to find me, this feeling was not completely new. This was the second time my kids and I weren't invited to Thanksgiving or welcomed to keep up with family traditions, and my spirit broke more. So when it happened again the feeling was familiar, but the pain hit differently. Six months after the text message, it was the first time we were invited over to my parents' house. There I sat with them, my cousin to my left sharing a couch, my mom on the love seat to my far right. My mother asked me what I was doing for Thanksgiving. And I replied, "Nothing, just going to be home." We were usually all together, so things clearly were changing. What I didn't realize in that moment was that plans had already been set and the consensus was that they "didn't want to make him uncomfortable." My brother's comfort overruled tradition and family. So I was eliminated. My husband, my kids and me.

I wasn't shocked by my cousin's behavior, though. Just 10 months older than me, she never grew out of her self-imposed and family-fueled competition with me. She was the angel, and I was the devil, which is ironic considering, in reality, she became the villain in my story. The person with the ability to be my bestest friend, my first example of a sister instead became a female version of the 1993 movie, The Good Son. The family sparked this dynamic with their comparison. Everything from labeling us "Gorda" y 'Flaca" to "Buena" y "Mala". But I wanted this relationship so bad. I knew my whole life I had a biological sister, but this person was the closest thing to that. I mean, shit, we were raised like twins. Our mothers were close and did just about everything together. They even dressed us alike with the same outfits, different colors. Just the most adorable thing ever!

We had so many opportunities to bond, even if it was through trauma. Neither of us knew our biological fathers, and we both had little brothers. We spent a lot of time together, every summer for years. We both had stepdads and crazy Puerto Rican mothers. I remember having sleepovers, playing together, and sharing the same interests in music. Then something changed when we hit adolescence. I want to say it was my promiscuity that bothered her most. I literally violated every girl code. We went to the same middle school, and she still lived on the other side of the Bronx but somehow her mom managed to get her to Riverdale from the Yankee Stadium area every day. I remember starting 6th grade and a boy named David started liking me. I believed she liked him too. But I am not sure if they actually dated. At the time he was with a girl whom I later fought with. My dad often reminded me that my cousin left me alone that day to fight. She didn't have my back.

Then there's the whole thing with my husband. I didn't accept that he was an issue between the villain and me until much later on. It all came together like a massive epiphany. Part of our love story is that we met through a male cousin over the phone and since she and I were together often, we would all talk on the phone. After speaking to him for a few weeks, we mailed him a picture of her, a childhood friend and myself. The picture was taken just under the 1 train on Broadway and W 231st Street. He chose her as the prettiest but also decided to catfish us before it was even a thing. He pretended to be one person with me and be himself with her. Did I realize then what was happening? No, of course not! It was all youthful, we were 11 and 12 years old and he was 14.

So here he was tricking us. I believe this went on for at least a month, if not slightly more. He confessed one day when she was at my house. I remember kneeling on the couch looking down from the 17th floor talking to him on the corded phone. When we asked him who he wanted to keep talking to, he chose me. I want to say it is because I was "hot in the box" but we're still going so maybe he made the right choice!

In March of 2022, she shared with everyone during a dinner celebration for my mother's birthday that my husband was her ex-boyfriend. And she was dead serious. My husband and I just looked at one another and laughed but there it was, the realization that almost 30 years later, the envious evil character is still competing with me. These are all just experiences I had to reflect on in an effort to understand the shift in a relationship I literally fought for verbally, emotionally and (in my dreams) physically.

I did not hear from her either after the life-altering text message. I had no communication until I took the kids to see my parents, and I hung out at her house, killing time. At this point, I had no beef with her, I also didn't know the narrative. She was not asking questions or disclosing anything either. Then a few weeks before my business ribbon-cutting in October of 2022, she called me insisting that I include her and allow her to contribute to my celebration. I was fine with her making cupcakes. She did an amazing and creative job. I mean the girl has awesome decor talent. She used margarita glasses to make cupcake stands.

Super cute, they were blue and right on brand! I loved it.

This was in October and by mid-November, I found myself texting her to ask why I wasn't invited to Thanksgiving, since my mom blamed her. My daughter is her goddaughter. I am the godmother to her son. So I did not understand why she'd insist on being present at a very special moment in my life and then ghost me. She ignored me. I texted again. Then, I sent a voice note. Nothing. So here I was, my mother telling me, "I only told her what your brother told me;" and, later being told, "I can assure you my niece has nothing against you."

I've become empathetic for her mentally comparative existence. As I approach the road of forgiving her I feel so bad for her. Always comparing yourself must be exhausting. I had the father-figure, the (allegedly) more stable mother, and the better sneakers (I have a vivid memory of her pointing this out). Then I had to go on and be cute and have a cute husband. In control of my life yet she never learned from me. Instead she compared her life to mine. I may never understand but it is not my job to. Other than what she can see on public pages she will never again be granted access to my life.

Have you ever noticed how someone who is horrible in one person's story can be a complete savior in another person's story? Love and the desire to be close prolonged the realization but this person was actually an evil character in my life story. It was a love/love, love/hate, love and tolerate your presence

68

relationship until I realized this person was the continuous villain. We all have them. I truly believe we experience different people at different points in their lives. As a person evolves, they change and are nothing like they were. I have learned this from influential speakers and coaches. It makes me think of those affected by the unhealed, mean, asshole versions of me. We project when we are lost and hurt. We are always making someone feel something, be it good or bad.

As I processed this shift, I compared how my first nuclear family treated her versus me. Disgusted that this was even a reality for me. Memories hurt more. I remember standing on my mother's porch. The four of us, mom, dad, me and lil' bro, and my dad saying, "It's just us." What a joke! Honestly, I felt replaced. I could not control that she fell more in line with my parents' expectations than I did. But I had to snap out of that mentality, it was not serving me at all. So, access had to be denied. This time I wasn't overwhelmed with the desire to be part of the family or control the narrative. My silence and absence felt more necessary. The last time I went through all the work, I forgave. I struggled knowing there were core values that differed between me and those I wanted most in my life.

And it's important to know that throughout this process you will feel all the feels. Sad, helpless, angry, invigorated and so much more. Feelings are ever-changing. This awareness requires a level of emotional intelligence. It is why we are advised not to make decisions while being emotional. Emotions are so telling, yet so volatile that it's hard to rely on them. A moment can stay with you, or it can go away until you see, smell, feel, hear or touch something. This is the depth of memory.

EVERYTHING comes back to our childhood. Our formative years, when we were learning the basics, our brain prepares and protect us. My method of protection was to remember the pain. It was my mechanism. Holding on to it so I never experience it again. Replaying it was the fuel to drive my life in a different direction. For example, being put out of the house at fifteen drove me to never go back, no matter how toxic my world was. Facing the double standard of having a baby at 15 and being put out yet seeing my brother with a child at 18 and being allowed to stay at home only added to my drive. Being an example to my daughter and proving so many people wrong drove me to be a high achiever. It was almost as if I needed these flames to keep my fire going.

Watching my grandparents and uncle slowly deteriorate mentally made me want The Notebook storyline. Don't we all want to be reminded about how awesome our lives and loves have been!? Despite the pain I will highlight throughout my life, I have had just as many happy, enormous love moments. So why not write about those? Well, the truth is the generational and cultural normalcy of certain things gets masked and embedded in the good times and good vibes. The obligation to create an external image of togetherness and unconditional love outweighs behavioral correction and accountability. It breeds narcissism and trauma. Lack of boundaries and misogyny get mixed in with jokes and lived experiences, so it all gets overlooked.

Having witnessed all this growing up, I am fascinated by the brain and its development. Understanding the importance and existence of it is vital and can truly assist in how we rear and interact with children. Studies have shown that a child's personality is developed between age seven and eight years old. The emotions, events, and experiences they have before they are teenagers is a major life contributor. We are all just little kids internally. We all carry the hurt and the moments that contribute to our responses and our relationships. So, to think that a child doesn't know or should stay in a "child's place" is ridiculous when you reflect on how their little brains are putting the pieces together at all times. Yet culturally, it is a standard.

We live in the time of "Woke" ideology yet crimes like sexual assault on minors and absentee fathers are still seen as "normal" in some families. One parent once told me, "It's okay, a lot of people grow up without their father." Yes, correct but that doesn't make it right and should not be normalized! There are countless studies and stories that speak to the effects of this circumstance; and everyone who takes part in the decision to accept this circumstance continues to contribute to these effects. The importance of it all is that we are a product of the choices originally made for us and around us combined with the choices we make for ourselves as adults. The beauty is that we are given free will in this life.

We hardly realize it until we make the distinct decision to believe something different than our parents or friends believe. We are taught family values and beliefs early on. Then, we take what we are given and try to figure out our place in the dynamic of the world in which we are born. The whole premise of nature versus nurture has been studied forever because both play massive roles. We are who we are, yet we try to fit in with who we are around.

Personally, I had to tap into all the foundations of faith that I knew. Growing up in a house where religion and faith were a mixed bag but a good foundation for a higher power faith really helped me. I grew up with Pentecostal godparents, a Catholic mother and a dad who classified himself as Protestant but never explained more than that. My mom always displayed faith around the house with Bibles, mini altars, and by cleaning the house with lucky leaves. I remember being sent to church as a punishment. "You gotta go to church," my dad shouted in the midst of his frustration with me. This is the same person whose opinion of my relatives was that they'd sin all week, then go to church to wipe themselves clean, just to do it again. Processing the dichotomy of the messages I was given made it super hard to believe God would solve fuckery with prayer. This was the beginning of what I later came to understand as the improper use of God, Jesus, faith, and the church. It was yet another reason I needed to reshape my matrix.

My commitment to being a godmother through the Catholic church kept me in relationships that no longer served me. I truly felt like a cursed godmother. I have baptized three children in the church with whom I now have no relationship. I have cried and continue to hurt over the discovery of subsequent choices. Unfortunately, we cannot control how others will respond to our hurt or our growth. We cannot save every relationship when it has run its course.

One of the last times I physically went to church was about a week before I went to Florida in 2018, before the re-traumatization. The sermon that day was different for some reason. It was a video about acknowledging, helping victims, and surviving sexual abuse. I sat there looking around wondering if I was the only one seeing an issue with this? The news, at the time, was being flooded of sexual abuse being exposed in the Catholic church yet here I sat getting an earful and visual about what should be done to help people like me. I was oblivious of the recent law change regarding the statute of limitations. The moment was ironic. In less than 2 weeks, I faced another community silencing victims and protecting predators. The whole ordeal shook my faith. I refused to simply pray about it. Yes, some things require us to "Let go and Let God", but not everything.

Coming to terms with drastic change is not easy but remembering that God removes people for a reason has been comforting. Embracing those whom He brings in to replace such absence is hard but necessary for growth. I had to brace myself for the impact because the internal turmoil was like wildfire. It is real. I battled and consciously lived by the standard, "When you know better, you should do better." But who determines what is "better"? Who says this is right or not? I have given grace to many but at what point do we start making changes? If you have had the pleasure of watching Disney's Encanto, you can see all the little things I am trying to highlight here.

There were family stories that no one was allowed to mention. It was an entire family cover up. Much like the well-known animated movie, they did not "talk about Bruno". Shame and pain surrounded the truth. Holding uncomfortable conversations and leading with love was not done but when does the cover up stop? Like Ed Mylett said, there comes a time when one person in a family lineage starts to question what is happening and what is considered normal. Just like Encanto's little Mirabel, I began to question the excuses made in front of me. Have you ever heard that one of the side effects of having learning delays or a handicap is calculatedly touching little boys and girls? I have NEVER heard of that. Yet this was the pacified story being told. It was the choice term used to mask the reality of the situation. The level of protection from all of the enablers and those who chose to "mind their business" kept the cover up going and opened the opportunity for more victims.

So how do you give grace to naive moments, a generational mentality and erred familial commitment, once they all know better? If you know you are wrong or that there is another way, rejecting it is a voluntary

74

act of denying the truth. It is a conscious effort to stay blind and accept fuckery. How does one get to the other side of that? I yelled bloody murder, begged to be seen, understood, and validated only to be told things would not change. "Let God." Let God do what now?

Sadly, knowing better doesn't always mean doing better in this dynamic due to blind loyalty. Blissful dysfunction has seemed to navigate the waters of family and loyalty. Turning a blind eye to a sexual predator is a huge ask of anyone yet it became normalized. The abandonment of a child became another normalized trait. As I run down my family tree, so many have been enablers or silent supporters of the enabler. I remember molestation being diminished to the excuses, "You know he's retarded" or "We can't break Abuela's heart." Only to find out Abuela was also a silent enabler and there were likely a lot more family victims. One male cousin got so tired of my rants that he blurted out, "No one has escaped him!" Another cousin defended this pedophile blindly, while one of his sisters pacified his actions by saying, "I will tell him to stay away from the pool in his complex because I know he's there looking at the little girls." Choices continued to be made to reinforce these fuckeries. Some people will never hear themselves or see how acceptance and silence breeds complacency and the ability for this sick person to do it again. It makes it so hard to forgive him because he is someone who is protected more than me by those we love. Somehow his actions, feelings, and motives are all explained and respected. Ironically, my emotional deliverance was always too much or deemed inaccurate.

Many people live their lives with a "minding my own business" mentality. This is healthy to some capacity. Like all things, it is about consistency. Selectively minding your business is not healthy nor is it consistent. The decision to give things energy is subjective. This is why content on meditating, mind control, and energy preservation are so prevalent these days. We are being told that we can control what and how we think. The art of compartmentalization and reconditioning your brain is fascinating. This is not an easy task for someone like me. When situations weigh heavy on my heart they seem to take over my mind. Have you ever felt that way?

Despite realizing in 2019 that my family lived in blissful dysfunction, I decided that having a relationship with my mother was still important to me. She is a good person, but Ed said, "It's not just about being a good person." Expecting her to know better and do better hindered that time in our relationship which contributed to the severance years later. I told myself that I took her as she was and understood that meant not agreeing with her, not liking everything but still wanting to be in her world and have her in mine.

She was critical but supportive, like most Puerto Rican mothers. Comforting but cold. I sympathized with the possibility that her mother rarely showed her what I was looking for in her. So, how could she know?! She too is a victim of tribal and cultural fuckery which is why her choice to put me out as a pregnant fifteen-year-old was not something I resented. I understood that it was her custom. She warned me consistently from the time I got my period, "You get pregnant, you get out." It is what she knew and, after not speaking to me for a few months, she did support me.

Early on, I chalked it up to the culture. My mother thought she was doing the right thing. There was a lot of what appeared to me as selective outrage. It may work for them but not us. It may work for my daughter but not my son. This gender can do that, but this one can't. This lack of uniformity became more apparent as more grandchildren were introduced to the family. Some fuckery was ignored, while others were called out.

I prayed then and most recently that she would be willing to have those necessary conversations with me. That she'd be willing to listen and see my hurt yet never lose sight that I appreciate her as a mother. Acknowledgement of me and my hurt is uncomfortable. To me, all of her efforts and her heart at its core made her an awesome mother on millions of levels. A lot of the choices, while questionable, only meant she's not perfect, and who is? Unfortunately, choices needed to be made in order to save myself, my truth and my mental well-being. I was adamant about the fact that certain narratives would NOT be a part of my story. So as hard as it was I had to let go of the remainder of my relationship with my mother after the text message. It was required in order for me to get to the other side and just maybe get a little closer to my purpose.

Chapter 6
Growing & Healing Hurts

So just hold on, ooh
Let time be patient
(You are still strong)
Let pain be gracious
"Hold On" - Adele

I struggled for a long time to find the words to talk to my parents again. I also feared that I would take too long to heal. I found myself crying sometimes, thinking, 'I miss my mom' or 'I miss my dad.' Yet, I am not sure if it was my pride or newfound boundaries that prolonged me from reaching out. There was still so much more sorting out I had to do emotionally. I could not be okay with small talk any longer. I refused to be silenced. I wanted answers, empathy, and comfort. I wanted accountability. However, what I wanted was not what I needed. I needed time. Time to sit with every event that I felt brought me to this moment. What was the lesson? What was the superpower I was supposed to take with me from the pain I was going through?

Suddenly, it was as if those around me were clueless, not knowing what to do when I was not complaining about my finances, my husband, or life in general. When my conversations shifted to increasing my credit score and saving money, the energy shifted too. Conversations with friends changed to reminiscing over the past. Distance was slowly created with those who no longer related to the shift and growth I was experiencing and displaying. Looking back to the toxic and immature times, I truly needed to hold on to grow graciously into the person I am slowly becoming every day.

Through the podcasts I listen to I have come to believe that, as you grow, people will start to become blind to your greatness. The purpose and reason you are in their world has ceased and they no longer see your light. This has allowed me to accept the absence of many people I love in my life and my children's lives. I have grown, I have boundaries, and most of all I know what I am not. This allows me to embrace the new people coming into my life who truly see my light.

When I decided to open my business during Covid, it was not expected of me. I wasn't even sure of it myself, but I did know that when I say I'm going to do something, I was going to do it. I wanted to finish high school, go to college, and go to law school, and I did! I was ambitious. I used to say, "I want my own practice by 40." Did I imagine that I would be a small business owner in a field I never thought of? No! I am and I have truly been blessed.

As Ed Mylett said when he discussed emotions, "We tend to gravitate to emotions we know, actions and customs as well." Watching my maternal grandmother run a small bodega in Puerto Rico during the summers

I spent there, I saw independence, inventory control, and a system of operation. From my godmother and mother, I learned motivational drive, dedication, and joy for life. I also saw connection, unity, support, hypocrisy, judgment, addiction, and love in the best ways they knew how. I caught the lessons and applied them to my life. All the things around a child are influential to their psyche. We never know what will stick.

Have you ever witnessed a child staring at you in the grocery store or in the waiting room of your doctor's appointment? Sometimes they just watch our energy or mannerisms. Around that same time, 10 or 11 years old, I stared at my mother in adoration thinking about how pretty she was. I'd play music I knew she liked just to see if she'd start vibing to it. I watched her work tirelessly. She instilled in me the mentality that money needed to be made. So much so that it was a rarity to see her struggling because she was always hustling to figure it out. Always keeping a job, working until late and coming home to cook dinner. Even if my dad was home for hours, the gender roles were real. We impact children simply by sharing a space with them. There was a saying I read once, "As a woman we influence other little girls even if we don't know them."

This phrase impacted me greatly and reinforced my firm belief that we are most influenced between the ages of 1 and 14. By 14, there is usually enough exposure. By 14, I already witnessed women battling demons, enduring abuse, and being independent. I watched my grandmother run her bodega and pack boxes of goodies for her kids to ship to the Bronx. I watched my godmother dedicate herself to her church, finish her degree, run her house and be a devoted mother. I watched my teachers, my aunts, my mother's friends and my friends' mothers. All these women played a role in my life. We take notes without realizing. They all influence who we become. My 5th grade teacher, Mrs. Irving made me feel seen and smart. I don't know if she saw a shift in me after the last molestation, but she hugged me when she saw me sad. I was tall, loud and so angry inside. She saw me.

Adults play a vital role in the lives of children for several reasons. Aside from providing necessities such as food and shelter to stay alive, adults provide guidance. Children are the victims and benefactors of adult decisions or silent partakers. This makes me think of the Bible verse from Ezekial 18:20, "The son shall not suffer for the iniquity of the father, nor the father suffer for the iniquity of the son. The righteousness of the righteous shall be upon himself, and the wickedness of the wicked shall be upon himself." The whole idea is understanding children can suffer the consequences of the choices made by their predecessors. While it may seem normal or communally accepted that does not mean it is or should be. It definitely doesn't work for everyone.

The truth is we are born into dynamics that we did not choose. Mother, father, siblings, aunts, uncles, etc. all compile what most call "family". I remember preparing a family tree in elementary school. Listing

81

everyone provided a hierarchy with labels. Yet those labels started to mean less and less to me as I began to discover who these people were as individuals. As egos, narrowmindedness or choices became more apparent, the labels started to hold less and less weight. At some point, I began to exhibit the "Thank you for wiping my ass as a baby but you're gonna respect me" attitude. Cutting people off became easier to do than to explain my boundaries and lack of participation in the acceptance of things I disagreed with.

In a lot of cultures and communities, speaking up for yourself and forming a boundary is seen as disrespectful. In my family, you would be called "Malcriada" (poorly raised or disrespectful) which I was called often in my adolescence. And I did everything to fulfill their "malcriada" label. My bad behavior with good grades was confusing. Being defiant with adults in my life was deemed embarrassing, having a baby at 15 was shameful, and my responses, emotions and existence were "too much". The narratives quickly believed about me, yet I pacified it by standing up for myself. Holding my head up high regardless of the shit being spoken behind my back and never to my face. It was as if everyone, up until the very end, avoided being real with me. I always over-share from my teenage years to now and I confide way too easily or naively think everyone has the same heart as me. I may have been too much to handle, but I know now that I was unique and different in a way those assigned to be my family were not familiar with.

I wanted and needed to go to the source and settle it. A conversation with a cousin summed it up when he spoke on behalf of the family by stating, "Everyone knows you, you're quick to curse people out, but you're good." Always disregarded with a subtle, "Oh, that's just Yari." Vocal, passionate, malcriada, disrespectful, extra – all terms used to describe me. Being my authentic and vulnerable self slowly came to feel as tolerated by all the people I love so much. I was quickly judged and labeled but loved.

"We can't expect from others what we know of ourselves," Jay Shetty said this in an interview once when he described fighting styles. Love languages are popular but the way we fight has yet to be given much attention. Jay spoke of his desire to address and face the issue at hand immediately whereas his wife did not respond that way to conflict. I related to Jay's approach. I am confrontational with a mindset of always wanting clarity and transparency which ironically is the entire premise of my small business. But this mentality also makes it difficult to let things go as you'll see as you read.

Shortly after I received the infamous text message and the painful weeks that followed, I continued to say, "They are not asking the right questions." It was evident to me that the stories circulating among others were accepted and there was no need for clarification or "the other side of the story". The conclusions were made, the wall was built, my dismissal and that of my husband and kids was just collateral damage. But to who's standard? Mine? Who was I to demand to be heard, to be seen? Who was I to demand fairness? I was in violation of the blind loyalty expected of me.

Yet, my loyalty and empathy previously allowed my truth to be muffled by their reality. Now I understand that my truth was questioned during a time when I began to learn who I was not and what I would not tolerate. Some choices I will never understand and the need to understand cripples healing. It can hinder growth and the path to forgiveness.

The problem is that moving forward without clarity can also feel crippling. You may be left to your own assumptions and answers. The better question is why do we insist on being heard and seen by those who refuse to? If answers were needed, questions would be asked. On the flip side, there may not be answers because the questions have never been asked. Having uncomfortable conversations is not common in my culture. Ultimately, facing me, or providing answers means challenging their reality.

I had to do something different. My pain slowly became my power. As I write these words, I am almost forty and the realization that I have been in this fight for so long is sad to me, depressing even. How much longer would I allow myself to suffer for the narrow mindedness of others? How long will it be okay to not speak up? When will I stop fighting for young me? When will my fight with ignorance turn into something that can benefit me or others?

As we grow, we find our voices and start making our own decisions. You begin to see it over the course of time. It continues to humble me as I get to know my children outside of needing me. They reveal my unhealed self and teach me when I sound ignorant. Growing up, I saw a lot of blended families around me. I myself had a stepfather and stepsiblings. I have an aunt with three baby daddies, another aunt and an uncle with an older child from a previous relationship. It was known and accepted. Having this foundation of blended families along with the continued addition of new members like girlfriends and babies contributed to the good heart I have. And it also fueled my motto, "Blood isn't thicker than water." In order to step away from those I shared blood with I had to lean into those with whom I did not share blood. Those were the ones who saw me most and loved me the way I needed to be loved in order to be my best self.

Chapter 7
A Renegade is Born

But there's a huge interference, they're sayin' you shouldn't hear it
Maybe it's hatred I spew, maybe it's food for the spirit
Maybe it's beautiful music I made for you to just cherish...
I'm a motherfucking Renegade
Renegade by Jay-Z Ft. Eminem

The black sheep. This may be someone you know. It may even be you! Every family has one. Oxford Dictionary defines it as "a member of a family or group who is regarded as a disgrace to it". I used to joke about being the black sheep because even as a teenager I knew I thought differently. I loved differently and expected to be treated differently.

Once the healing starts to happen, the way you process words and actions change. You no longer take misogynistic jokes the same. You no longer tolerate racism or ignorant comments around you. That is what happened to me. I would quickly point out if something didn't sound right. One of the first things I noticed was the expectation of gender roles. It was evident from early on that the woman cleans, cooks, and handles domestic work even if she worked outside of the home. It wasn't until later in life that I saw my dad do some laundry, cook, and clean a bit. My brother was not expected to cook or clean at all. As my only son got older, I began to break generational norms by teaching my son to cook and clean. My dad once offered to pay me to not have my son do dishes. He said, "Have him throw out the garbage." While it was funny, I noticed he was serious, and gender roles were taken seriously too.

Culturally, men were expected to cheat. If a woman did the same, she was a whore. Growing up, I heard stories about how my grandmother and another woman both found themselves pregnant at the same time, a lot of the time. My Abuela, being a working woman, would have the other woman watch her children. I joked with my mother that it was their version of sister wives. The acceptance of this behavior was only doubled down as traditions, and this mentality was passed down. We have heard the stories of men who have more than one family. There is a great song that highlights the truths of it, "Papa was a Rolling Stone" by the Temptations.

When my husband and I hit the roughest time in our marriage, we both had affairs. My mother barely talked to me, silently judging me. My dad would say things like, "He is a better man than me, I can't play in the sandbox if someone else played in my sandbox." They judged us. They talked about us being ridiculous cheaters and gave us little credit for working past the fixed mentality around infidelity. I did not want my children to believe these things. Neither men nor women should be expected to cheat. Nor should anyone feel immune to infidelity. Most importantly, it does not necessarily mark the end of a relationship.

There is something about the black sheep though. Their words seem to hold as much darkness as those who see them as the problem. Their words are not heard, they easily fade into the stories that others want to repeat and believe about them. We are the ones that question why things are the way they are. We demand clear answers. We find ways to improve the future for ourselves and those we love. We are driven to change the way the world sees people like us.

It took a long time for me to shake off the stigma of the label, Black Sheep. I now see it as a quality. I worked hard not to be a statistic but also to be an example that a black sheep is nothing more than a person who is misunderstood and silenced. It wasn't until college that I learned about memory loss and its association with trauma. In applying my own life to my studies, it was very apparent that I had a handful of memories and the majority of them are associated with trauma or fuckery. I was convinced that I lost my memory due to all the trauma I experienced. The most vivid one was at 5 years old, one I have tried to forget. I remember lying on that bed as a child being violated by a man who was labeled my uncle. I remember sharing it with my mom the next morning while she sat on the toilet. I remember feeling like I did something wrong because my parents were so stressed. But life went on. No therapy, no talking, no consequence.

As a parent I cannot imagine what my parents were thinking. I still remember those moments as if they just happened. Snippets of the violation when I was 5 and the entirety of the one when I was 10. The immediate consequences after the first molestation incident was hypersexuality at only 5 or 6 years old. Shortly after that, at 7, I made out with a boy who went to my church. After we moved to Virginia Beach for a brief time, I changed my name to Jennifer. Everyone respected that I wanted to be called Jennifer. The entire time I lived there, I was Jennifer. Our first day there, I met a neighbor who was about five or six years older than me. I lied and told him I was 11 but he found out I was 7 because I was in his little sister's class. His family became our friends, and I was able to spend the night often. The first time I did, I initiated the conversation. I was ready. One night he sat next to me but made it clear he would not be having sex with me.

Do you ever think back to things you endured and think I wish you could hug your younger self? Tell him or her it will be okay. I would tell little Yari that being touched by a family member was not okay and that it resulted in hypersexuality that everyone around refused to acknowledge. That this confusing time will eventually become your power.

At 10, the association with beer was the lingering trigger of the trauma. You see, he was an alcoholic. The so called "uncle" smelled and tasted like beer. It took me a very long time to control the trigger. The brief kiss that man gave me stood with me for decades. I still do not drink beer, and I stayed away from wine until my mid-thirties because it smelled too much like beer to me. I am not sure how that particular day came to be. I just know I had a key to let myself into the house. And when I did he was lying on the couch, visible as soon as I opened the door. I immediately had a gut feeling that I did not want to be around him. When I closed the door, he woke up, saying "You're not going to give me Bendicion?"

Bendicion is a cultural norm where the child requests an elder's blessing with the word "Bendicion" and the adult replies, "Dios te bendiga," (God bless you). Not doing this is seen as disrespect. I walked reluctantly toward him, and he kissed my cheek over and over until he got to my mouth and tried to tongue kiss me. I pushed him away and his drunk ass ended up slumping again. I left, went downstairs to my friend's house where I stayed until I knew my dad would be home. When I walked in, I was yelled at, "Why did you leave, where were you?" But that man was sitting there on the couch, so I said nothing. I was scared. The next day I told my mom that he had kissed me with tongue. Another episode of shock and uproar ensued and then it was over. I remember my dad being pissed. He later told me my mom begged him not to hurt her brother.

That event may have triggered the family's decision to ship him to Puerto Rico, which is where I saw him next, living with my grandparents. When I was 13, I was sent there for the summer as a response to my rebellion with no thought about the fact that this man would be around me. Maybe they knew by that point that I was not his type. I was too old. By the time I met my first boyfriend at 11, I was super-promiscuous. It was deep puppy love. I trusted him with every part of

90

me. We had deep conversations. He lost his dad at a young age, and his mom was a strict Boricua who was best friends with my Titi. They lived a block and a half away from one another, making it super convenient for me to see my boyfriend. I was "culeca" (always excited and mischievous), like Boricuas say. He and I were dreamers. We were both 13 by the time making out was not enough for me. He was scared, naturally! Within 6 months, I lost my virginity to someone else, slept with a 19-year-old at 13, and attempted suicide. I was on a fast track of fulfilling all the labels placed on me until I met my future husband.

Meeting my future husband changed the course of my life. We were young, passionate, toxic and in love. Over two and a half decades later, I now joke that it is a healthy obsession. At the time it was a necessary obsession because it kept me focused. It wasn't until after we had our first daughter that I began to process the trauma of the sexual abuse I endured. It began to affect my sex life drastically. I would cry spontaneously and feel creeped out while he touched me. The sixteen-year-old me was finally processing because I had begun therapy with Martha. School was my escape and safe haven. I didn't know it then, but my healing journey was beginning.

At 19, I was slapped with the reality of fuckery. I confronted my family with it all, while in Puerto Rico for my Abuelo's funeral in 2005. A late-night discussion led to the topic of becoming a mom at 15, which then led to my mother's remark, "It's not my fault you were promiscuous." I reacted by telling her, "No, it is you and your brother's fault." That night, in the heat of it, I called my dad who was in NY at the time, and he said, "You let him in." I yelled, "No I did not!" That's not how I remembered it.

As a growing and healing adult, it saddens me because many people knew what happened. And if the family didn't know before, they knew now that I was sexually molested as a 5-year-old and then at 10 years old. Many spoke privately about it, but everyone ultimately did nothing. Thereby silencing the victim and enabling the violator to do it again which he did. When I became vocal about it I was told "get over it", or "he's retarded." I was repeatedly victim shamed as a teen and again after he retraumatized me as an adult. This man, my violator, was brought to live in the same house I lived in when I was seven. He needed a place to live and my parents agreed to it. If he violated me then he'd be homeless. He did not molest me at that time, but when the roof over his head was not at jeopardy, he took advantage. This reality is what convinced me that he was not "retarded" as his supporters and enablers claim. He's calculated.

My entire experience with him was overlooked and forgotten that night in 2018. My healing went unseen up until that point. I was expected to share a porch with this man, who touched my little girl vagina and made me touch his grown man penis with my five-year-old hand, at the Airbnb where we hung out.

Here we were at a family event with a man preying and grooming while everyone else enjoyed the great music and open bar. Other partygoers and

92

relatives failed to notice him with my little cousins conversing in the lobby of the party we attended in Tampa, Florida. I interrupted them at one point, as partygoers went in and out of the venue. Sending the girls inside, away from him. I took a mental note of the interaction but kept partying. I was childless and on vacation. He was later seen touching and kissing one of those children. As she innocently sat at a table with her head down on the table, this man proceeded to kiss her cheeks and lift her dress.

That night I was told, "I thought you were stronger than that." Seriously? Was I expected to be strong enough not to react to him violating another child? I was retraumatized. Believe it or not, the violation is less painful than the way it was handled. He took my innocence, but the family's continued silence affected me more. I refused to return home with my parents after that trip. They didn't talk to me. The narrative was that I disrespected my mother and caused a show. My brother called me a little over a week later to say, "You are hurting dad, why did you even go?" This was the first time we were not invited to participate in holiday festivities. It hurt me badly but I only lasted three months standing on my boundaries and principles.

It was like bargaining in the grief process. I knew then that I was definitely different from my family. I knew there were morals and ways of thinking I could never understand but I wanted them in my life more. I had to find a way. After a long text message to my mom was well received and a response that I felt was an authentic apology, we went back to being a family. I made the decision to overlook our very distinct beliefs.

Whenever you overcome a huge hurdle in a relationship, you are typically pleased and at ease. I truly thought we had overcome the biggest thing we would ever have to face. There were things I went along with for the sake of family. But shutting out a child was not one I could get behind. My brother's second daughter came into my life when I was more healed than any other time in my life. Another narrative was spun to change the events from how they undoubtedly occurred. Neutrality was the choice word many used in an attempt to "mind their business". Conversations were had, a consensus was reached, and everyone moved on. I could never imagine my parents being okay with me having a piece of shit baby daddy who refused to see my kids. They would have talked shit from here to forever! Selective oblivion and outrage.

Culturally, the boys are just not expected to do much more than be cute. If they are losers, pedophiles, or anything in between it is pacified. This only pushed me to want more for myself, but I judged them for not putting that same pressure on my brother. I never compared the discrepancies in their parenting more than when we both already had children. I once asked my dad why they were so hard on me compared to my brother. When I brought home a 90, I was told it could have been 100. While my brother's "barely passing" grade was acceptable. When I stole something, I got whipped. He was only shamed for getting caught. So what was the answer to my question? My dad simply replied, "We expected more from you."

And this is why, even as an adult with children, I was still questioned and pressed for just about everything. Questioned and criticized for everything from my acne to my home renovations. The lack of pressure and accountability is clear when you dig deep into the inconsistent decisions that are made. The inconsistency was even evident in how my husband and my brother were treated. My husband came into my family when he was 16 years old and my dad gave him a hard time all the time. He expected more from him too, I guess. My dad would curse my husband out for almost everything, constantly telling me he wasn't shit and couldn't really take care of his young family. Then he would love on him and teach him plumbing, horse racing, and music. He instilled a lot in him and influenced him quite a bit. Yet he never applied the same pressure to his own son. The requirement to take care of your kids, which was a frequent conversation, was not of a uniform standard. This lack of discipline was definitely a contributing factor to my brother's decision to send me that text message in 2022. Not being held accountable is a continuous toxic element that is seen throughout these family dramas. Pacifying actions and silencing the person looking for clarity or understanding follows.

No matter how hard I tried, I could not wrap my mind around the mentality that having an absentee biological father was no big deal. Not knowing your birth father was continuously becoming more acceptable. My mother grew up with a fairly absent father. Both my Bio and dad did not know their fathers either. I have cousins that have no relationship with their fathers. But I am here to tell you that it matters. It truly matters. A child will start to put the pieces together and wonder how they fit into this dynamic called "family." Just like I always wondered about my biological father. I longed for him until I became angry with him.

After I found out about him and his passing, I mourned him. And today, I embrace the relationship I have with him beyond the grave. I hold dear the stories shared with me about his attempts to know me. I learned that he would bring me up in conversation and wonder about my existence. I also remember my dad sharing that he took the pictures he saved for me of my Bio out of the garbage and told my mother he would hold them for me. He always made me feel that he had my back like no one else.

I had many conversations with my dad about the narrow-minded thinking of my mother's side of the family. My dad stood up for me a lot so when we were estranged, it killed me deeply.

Honestly, I never felt like a stepchild until the text message. My dad always had a way of making me feel like he knew me, he saw me. I'm forever grateful for the foundation and realness my mom and dad provided. My parents began dating when I was almost 2 years old. My first memory of him is walking in the hallway of the Bronx River projects. I was about five years old. We rode in the elevator up to his mom's apartment at Bronx River projects. He reached out for my hand as we exited the elevator, and he asked me if I was okay. We walked down to the last door on the left and I remember feeling safe. My bond with him increased after that moment. He became my dad. My appreciation for his presence has become almost overwhelming at times. Fueled by reminders that my life would have been very different had he left. At the same time, his chosen words made me respect my mother less. It produced this feeling, as if my mother did not put me first or care to understand me.

Having a great father figure, by far, remained the one privilege I never took for granted. I often would think about how my life would have turned out had my mother not met my stepdad. How would it have been if he had not stuck around? These facts charged my appreciation even more. Yet, not knowing about my Bio was a void. You may know that girl, the one with the "Daddy issues"? I was that girl. You may even be that girl. The worst is knowing a little girl right now going through that. That feeling of abandonment, neglect, and dismissal. I was the little girl who wondered about her biological father too. I did not want this to be a part of my story. And deep down, my family knew it too, which is why they were selective with what was shared with me.

The little girl in me who suffered from those actions and choices was healed enough to allow grace and embrace those I love as family. I know you are probably thinking, 'Hell no!' After being silenced for so long, fighting to make it right, you probably would have

97

given up a long time ago. I had to experience the other level of fuckery that triggered the little girl who desperately wanted answers about the other half of me. That little girl became an angry and rebellious young lady. I was a little girl who had a good father-figure but still felt an absence and it took two years after finding out my biological father had passed for me to stop "looking" for him.

I was selective in what I shared with my family after 2018 too. I decided to maintain a connection with my niece when no one else did. I chose to ask questions when the entire topic was added to the "Bruno" list. There I was allowing myself to be silenced again. It was better than the alternative for a while. Allowing yourself to go down the rabbit hole and rationalize the actions of narrow minded and unhealed people is crippling! All you can do is decide if you will take part in it or not. I was asking myself the wrong questions for a long time. I was trying to wait for time to make it better, avoiding the topic to keep the peace, working on minding my business when in reality I had to go deeper.

Do the people you spend your most precious time with share your values? Was my way of thinking and who I was becoming so far off from those with whom I got here? Am I bugging out? In these situations, you will experience anger with all of this confusion. It is the beginning of grieving relationships. Anger is a huge part of grief. Grieving individuals who are still alive is even harder. It's natural and yet bargaining with small doses of these relationships so you don't lose them or give up on them is not conducive to your healing. Many times I felt that I needed to stay angry in order to get through and not give in to the little girl longing for her mother's love and inclusion or the relationships and friendships I convinced myself would be for a lifetime.

Everyday is so different in this process of acceptance. But do we ever really accept? Why are we meant or asked to accept anything? Acceptance in Merriam Webster is defined as being able or willing to accept something or someone; the readiness or willingness to accept or adapt to a given circumstance. I don't think we have to accept anything that you know is not meant for your destiny or does not align with who you want to be, or what you believe is your purpose. I was suffering in many ways whether expressed or silenced. As shifts occurred and boundaries were placed, I gained my voice back.

In the days and weeks following the text message, I felt lost. One day in one of those "OMG I am losing my mind" moments, I stepped out into my backyard, looked up into the beautiful June sky, and closed my eyes tight. Holding in my rage and my tears. I breathed in and out and spoke to God. I just asked Him for strength because I was so confused, I felt beat up. When I opened my eyes, I looked around and as my eyes began to focus, I looked at my fence and noticed a dragonfly. Not one but five! I took it as a sign that I would be okay. I am okay. From that moment, at any given time throughout spring, summer and fall, I was surrounded by dragonflies. They appear as soon as I step outside, almost slapping me! I've even had one try to get into my car three times. It is surreal.

At the most mentally-challenging and emotionally weak moments throughout this painful time, they just appeared. So I tattooed it! Look for signs. I began to be grateful for the smallest things that are actually huge like vision, ability and breath. Verbalizing the little things you're grateful for or creating a mental checklist of them helps reduce the list of the things you are not so grateful for. Shifting my focus from what I am missing to what I have and taking the dragonflies as a sign was pivotal to healing.

After a few years went by, I decided to look up the meaning of the dragonfly and learned that they represent growth and change. Dragonflies represent transformation, and isn't that what life is about? Constant transformation. If you ever get to a point where you think you have nothing more to learn, where you think that laying back and scrolling or just existing is better, then you are not living. You must continue to grow in some way. Mentally, spiritually, emotionally, financially, or any other way necessary to improve your quality of life is needed to continue to fulfill your purpose. Like Ed says, "You are meant to do something great." But GREAT doesn't happen while refusing to learn. Change does not happen without acknowledgment, accountability, and uncomfortable conversations.

Allowing myself to cry helped a lot as well. I was feeling pain, not just for myself, but for my children. I do not know how they processed the estrangement. On my part, I tried my best not to speak loudly or around them at all. I was a walking ball of hurt. I know they saw it, regardless of my efforts. When the rush of emotion rises it's easy to tell yourself, "F that, I don't need this," and compartmentalize the feeling. But is that really helpful? I'd stuff my face in my bed and yell and cry the ugly cry. In the middle of listening to Salsa music, I would start crying and thinking, 'I miss my mom.' It was such an abrupt change. Going from speaking every day, multiple times a day to nothing.

Distance doesn't reduce the reality of the pain. I began drinking a lot more, which didn't help my mental processing either. Listening to music has been extremely therapeutic for me but it also triggers memories of good times and shared moments. Having those fun, priceless memories are a blessing and a nice part of my entire life story. Every good moment with these people in your life, that you have loved all your life, makes you who you are now. Hold on to those moments. They are precious. Most families with deep generational traumas and fuckery include amazing love and people who have the best intentions for their loved ones. They too are not well from their traumas. They too are limited due to exposure and crippled from the conditioning they have received. I encourage you to cherish every part that was amazing in your childhood. It will make you a better person tomorrow because you can slowly accept that most people who shaped who you are did the best they knew how.

Chapter 8
Growing Out of the Labels

You can say I am the same but
I adjusted to all the hurt
Sometimes - H.E.R

My mother met my biological father (who I call my Bio) during a time when she was just "having fun". She thought he was dreamy. His height, smile and light eyes captivated her. She didn't expect him to stick around so she was happy that it was just her and me until she started dating my dad, the man who slowly became my father figure from the age of eighteen months. One of the two pictures of my Bio that they kept for me was of him standing in the bedroom holding me up with his hands while he kissed my head. The angle was of someone sitting and looking up, so it captured his height and slinkiness. His hair looked amazing in it, an afro puff. I was less than three months old. The other picture was of me on the bed, and he was sitting next to me. He looked up at the camera with his pretty features, laying his hand next to his infant. They were precious pictures, and it was extremely thoughtful to keep those for me.

I didn't come to know the story of how my mother met my biological father until I was much older. My mother made sure I knew I had a sister on my Bio's side and that her name started with a J. I was able to put pieces of the story together through a series of different conversations over the years while hanging out and drinking among family. After age eight, I was obsessed with finding more Matos family members. I remember, in middle school, I would hang out in my guidance counselor's office. One day, I went through his files to see if I saw a person with the same last name. I was the only Matos I knew except for my cousin's dad but I dismissed that relation because he was of Dominican descent and my mother told me certain facts to which I held fast.

No matter what, I always lifted my mother's title above all. After all, that is what we are taught - obey thy mother and father. In my culture, respecting your elders is mandatory. Even if you didn't know them. The title they held in the hierarchy earned them automatic respect and acknowledgment of respect. I was well aware early on about my privileges. Growing up in the projects with my friends who were less fortunate instilled this self-awareness in me. We all suffered when there was no hot water or when the elevators were broken but simply walking into my childhood apartment, it was clear based on how it was kept and our belongings that we were more fortunate, and my parents were hard-working.

Being raised in the projects, having to step around piss spots, dealing with broken or stinky elevators, walking up several flights of stairs, all of that, I think humbled me. I had exposure to what poverty was through my friends and my mom's friends who lived very poorly, much poorer than us, because when we stepped into our apartment, we had the best of the best all the time.

My mother's drive and capacity to make things happen is really why I think I'm the way I am. It also stems from my grandmother who was an entrepreneur and always worked. She wasn't very nurturing or motherly, but she was a doer. And you can see that trait in each of her daughters' personalities.

So, I always knew I was fortunate, and I was grateful. But eventually, gratitude outweighed the discrepancies, hypocrisy and inconsistencies. Gratitude started to feel like it was suffocating me. Remember how I mentioned earlier that we are born into dynamics we do not choose? And I said that we are placed in a hierarchy of family members with labels; labels which I took very seriously. At the advice of one of my sisters, I began removing the labels of the people I love. I had to remove the "given birthright". The bloodline label that came with this human experience. This removal allowed me to see each character for their individual self. I saw the person for who they were – their ways, their choices, their mindset and values. This unmasking reduces the boundary of unquestionable respect that is heavily embedded from childhood. It allows you to see a person as a fellow human rather than the labeled person whom you're told to respect and obey by all means socially, culturally and religiously.

When you start removing these labels, continuously remind yourself of who you are not and why those ways and mindsets no longer serve you. It does not get better with time. It gets better with acceptance. Acceptance that we cannot change or control everything, much less a person. Accepting that their choices are not personal rather they had to make them for their own mental perseverance. These individuals may be a walking ball of trauma and negativity. They may lack emotional maturity. They may have had their heads gassed up for so long that they truly think they can speak or behave in any way without consequences. But the major consequence is no longer having access to you.

If you take their choices personally then the removal from your life is a blessing as they no longer see you. It's hard not to have expectations. I find this stage to be the hardest and it creates the biggest rollercoaster of emotions. Wanting what we want but knowing it's not good for us. Cue Meghan Trainor's song, "Bad for Me". The lyrics speak of a desire to express your pain yet doing so would be useless. Literally a pain to the heart that causes nausea. It wrenches deep to the soul. It's natural to want our parents to embrace and love us. There is no other way of explaining it. Either way, processing a loss like the expectations of a parental relationship is not an easy task. I, myself, continue to struggle with wanting a relationship with my parents. And currently, the existence of a relationship is because the amount of gratitude I have is so much bigger than my sadness and hurt. The desire for a relationship doesn't correct the wrong nor ease the reality of the fuckery. It is all the yo-yo of grief where you compromise the pain to keep the family familiarity.

Letting people back in your life or evaluating how much weight they hold in your life is an adjustment. We must adjust and learn. Learning how much to engage and which conversations to have is tricky. One thing I have adopted and will continue to embrace as I heal is understanding who I am not. It is quicker to identify what you are not willing to tolerate than identifying what you will based on who you're not. We can confidently say I am not okay with A, B, C. I will not support D, E, F. These declarations do not have to be concrete because, most of the time, we make declarations based on what we know, and that knowledge may be limited. At the same time there are some boundaries, declarations and moral guidelines that are non-negotiable. As you learn who you are and become who you are meant to be, it is okay to shift your way of thinking. It is okay to be different. It is what makes you unique. Identifying these things has facilitated my boundaries and allowed me to get to know myself more. You can do it too!

Chapter 9
Transforming Pain

Blessings on blessings on blessings
Look at my life man,
that's lessons on lessons on lessons
Blessings - Big Sean

Why do we feel the need to prove ourselves to people? Isn't it ironic how we fight to be seen by those who already have their concrete view of us? Why not allow yourself to be seen and loved by those who already see and love you? Rather than those who say they love you, but whose actions don't align. It is refreshing to be around those who see your value and contribution towards making the world a better place.

A soul can come into your life, give you what they are meant to give, and seemingly destroy that purpose if they overstay their necessity in your life. What do I mean by this? The reasons, seasons, and lifetime people – they are in your life for a reason, a season, or a lifetime. We have to figure out which one because a person can come into your life to support you and teach you but, if they overstay their purpose, they can tarnish the reason. You must place the characters in your story accordingly. Some are not meant to be in every chapter of your life for the rest of your life.

This was a hard lesson to learn especially when it came to friendships. Some of these people were the closest to me and they were supportive during painful times of my life, but they were not going to be the people to take me to the next level of my growth. I was a different person. Some days it feels super sad, but you have to go through, not around, to get the other side of this pain. I just may be meant to go through this in order to meet the stronger version of me. Just like me, there are people who are suffering in silence, refusing to heal out loud because they want to hold on to relationships they have outgrown.

Have you had a relationship that just didn't fill your cup like it used to or maybe stopped filling it altogether? A lot of the relationships I had before 2020 consisted of conversations that lacked growth. I was always on the trajectory of improving my life, but I rarely discussed it. I never went deep into my schooling or financial goals for myself with anyone. Most of my conversations surrounded my nuclear family or my unhealed parts. The phrase "'outgrowing relationships" sticks out to me as I write. In fact, Tyler Perry's concept rings as the best solution to making peace with this inevitable reality through human experience. Perry once discussed comparing people in his life to the different parts of a tree. Some are branches, leaves, or roots. Each plays a vital role in the life of that tree but one thing about a tree is that it is ever changing and adapting to its elements. So why as humans do we expect our lives to be consistently the same?

The designated role of your parents in your life may have been to bring you onto this earth, nothing more. That may have been their only assignment concerning you. Expecting more based on cultural and social guidelines can affect the relationship going forward. In other words, when we remove the label and understand the capacities or lack of capacity a person has, regardless of the title we put on them, it can reduce the pain from unspoken expectations. Making sense of this becomes a bit more complicated when you take the same parent and apply their ways to two different children. I have seen this in how the first-born child is reared compared to the ones that follow. I see it in my own child rearing. There are things I would never have allowed with my first born but with the second and third it's different because they are receiving a different version of me.

It may take a while to adjust to this reality, so it has to become about giving yourself grace. The plan is to get stronger everyday and love yourself. Standing in your truth, your dignity and values matter more than the hierarchy. It is painful though. Ripping yourself apart from a big part of your identity feels horrible. Being unapologetic about choosing to change, however, can feel empowering. Burning the bridge or ripping the cord was a necessary step to begin the journey of becoming a better version of myself. It was needed to begin the painful process of becoming who I am destined to be. So many people brought so much value for so long, but

I had to grow beyond that. And almost none of them knew what to do with me so I easily became the problem. I was labeled as dramatic and emotionally reactive when in reality I was beginning to form boundaries as I discovered who I was not and what I would not allow around me.

It's important to understand that not everyone will receive your story or decisions with positivity. We don't hear enough about how it feels; like going up the down escalator - exhausting. The key is to remember for whom you are sharing your story. In the thick of it, during a networking meeting, I shared with a "stranger", a work client, about my mother. I shared that I was molested. It bothered me immediately after because I had not allowed myself to be that vulnerable with someone who didn't know me personally for a while. Their response was, "People need you." This isn't the first time I have heard this. Ed said, "We wake up everyday because someone somewhere needs us." We need to share our lives, our hurt, our human experience to help them, in the words of this colleague, "not be stuck."

Are there certain expressions you say to yourself that help course-correct your thoughts? "Necessary challenges" is the phrase I continuously told myself to get through some days. A challenge is the only way to grow and change. Children studying in school increase in levels because challenges are increased throughout the year to move them up. This same concept applies to life when navigating emotionally, mentally and spiritually. Since schools lack this education, we have to learn this ourselves and teach children how to interact with others, express themselves and find peace within themselves. We may see the day when mental and emotional health are addressed more.

It's amazing how free you feel when accepting the things you cannot control. It's not easy. It's almost as if you have to recondition your brain and emotions to adjust to your new life and new connections. After reading Ed's book, *The Power of One*, I've learned that we must change and that we are always making people feel something. Awareness is the major lesson I've learned. Working on forgiveness with acceptance, not accepting the actions or decisions but accepting that their reality no longer serves me. Accepting the season of their presence and the blessing of their absence. Sometimes you don't know your boundaries until you're faced with them.

I was a new person, this pain transformed me. Before June of 2022, I called myself an "anti-pet" person and would have bet money that I'd never ever have a dog. I did not want the responsibility and possibility of a tragic heartbreak that usually accompanies a hefty vet bill. Everyone knew this as I was adamant and vocal about it when my husband announced his desire to have a dog. Yet, I do not think it is a coincidence that I got a dog during what I now consider one of the most painful times of my life. He came less than two weeks before Christmas Eve 2022. That morning I woke up with the epiphany that I did not deserve to be treated like this by "family".

Getting a dog changed my perspective, my life, my energy and my being. I spent the first two to three months saying and thinking, 'I can't believe this is my life.' But it has become an amazing part of my life. He brings me joy like I never imagined. He allows me to slow down and enjoy life, his personality, and the pure love of companionship. All the people who exited my life in 2022 know nothing about the dog mom in me. They do not know the girl who can't wait to talk about him. I once saw a meme that said, "God gave you a dog to apologize for the shitty relatives you have." That phrase hit me so hard. Those words made so much sense. God knew I had so much love and it needed to be placed somewhere.

My summer and my weekends looked really different very quickly. It feels wrong. It feels lonely. It feels dismissive. Yet the dragonflies and my dog kept me going, always there giving me reminders that it's okay. I've joked that God knew I needed a place to transfer all this love and good times! I now shop intently for my dog, he makes my day but can get on my dang nerves, like a child. He is a drooling expense that I love to pieces. I even baked a cake for him for his birthday, which was the first time ever making a cake from scratch. The lesson I learned was "never say never". Life takes you through moments that may shift your entire understanding of who you are and what you need.

You truly never know what God's plan is or what the future holds. Your life can change quickly and dramatically. You can find yourself doing and saying things you could never imagine. I am learning to embrace this. I hope to encourage those who find it impossible to try it. I believe the only way I have managed to get this far without completely losing my shit in an emotional rage is by surrendering to the reality that this is how it is supposed to be. I can only control myself, my responses and, progressively, my emotions. It is not an easy task, but it diminishes the pity.

It's empowering to be able to control the way you feel. Increasing the "quality of your life," as Ed says. It truly is about finding ways to shift your mind and resources to empower you. I went from listening to Eminem to comfort my anger with songs like "Cleaning out my closet" and "Who Knew" to listening to podcasts that have promoted my growth and mental health. Have you ever felt like you had to hold on to something painful or replay it in order to stay in that emotion? It is a defense mechanism that is crippling to only you.

As I write this book and truly process the life experiences that have brought me to this moment, the continued emotion that rises is gratitude. I can spew stories that would make anyone bitter and angry, yet I have chosen not to hold on to those moments. I appreciate them. The moments that are deeply troubling like being molested and silenced by relatives slowly become less nauseating. Instead, they empower me more and more.

As a part of my spirituality, since Covid, I watch and listen to a church online, Fresh Start Church, headed by Apostle G. Morris Coleman and located in

Mount Vernon, New York. Thanks to an old coworker (now friend), who sends me the link every week. During one sermon, Apostle Morris said, "This is happening to you but it ain't about you." Those words hit my soul and have now become a part of my mantra. It gives my life a different purpose due to how I am perceiving the things I am going through.

Embracing this mentality allows the opportunity to learn from your experiences versus viewing yourself as a victim of your circumstances. Like I tell my children, it is okay to be upset, sad, or annoyed. Feel the feeling but don't stay stuck. Feelings shift, sometimes quicker than a squirrel running up a tree which is why most people would advise you not to make decisions when upset or emotional. Have you ever said things or acted in a way that is so out of character due to a feeling? This is why there are crime classifications like crimes of passion. The passion and intensity that can arise from emotion can have lasting effects. Emotional maturity is required and an uphill climb to learning.

When you're working on emotional maturity, what you watch and listen to affects your psyche. When I opened my business I understood the importance of social visibility. I opened up social media pages with a promise to control my algorithms as much as I can. Why allow my phone to make me feel a way about myself or my life? It becomes part of your matrix like Ed Mylett said, "You choose your matrix."

When I give a little peek into my experiences as a teen parent, I get emotional. It wasn't easy. There were a lot of barriers, challenges and distractions and, yet I didn't feel it at the time. Ed says, "You usually don't know you are doing something great while you are doing it." I am not the lone example, but I am rare. We have to allow ourselves to embrace the uniqueness of ourselves without having an ego boost. Our stories can help others. When I reflect on the days of taking two buses, going up a long steep hill and a long set of stairs with my baby as a teenager, I don't think, 'Hell yeah! I did that.' I think, 'Wow, I am so grateful I could.' I am grateful for the support of a roof over my head and the ability to get an education. I always wanted and still want to be an example to my kids that this human experience isn't easy, but we are capable of kicking ass and not allowing ourselves to be victims of our circumstances.

Believing I can empower my pain makes me feel like I had to endure the hypocrisy, double standards, generational mess, heartache, and disappointment to reach this point, though far from where I want to be. I've wanted to help young girls who can benefit from knowing certain chapters and challenges I've overcome as a teen mother. I never wanted to share my story so as not to make anyone look bad because honestly these snips of experiences, from my perspective, don't make these people bad. To them, I was the drama-filled, passionate, emotionally reactive person who complained about her job, marriage, and kids. What will they do now that I am talking about building an empire, embracing gentle parenting, calling fuckery what it is - fuckery? How can they navigate my truth when it threatens their reality?

Chapter 10
Healing Out Loud

It's just the way it is
And maybe it's never gonna change
But I got a mind to show my strength
And I got a right to speak my mind
And I'm gonna pay for this
They're gonna burn me at the stake
But I got a fire in my veins
I wasn't made to fall in line
No, I wasn't made to fall in line, no
"Fall in Line" - Christina Aguilera ft Demi Lovato

We change with every experience, and I have extended grace to my parents knowing they did their best with what they knew. The hump is selective application of knowledge based on cultural norms and the acceptance of fuckery but not everyone is your assignment. You are not meant to encourage or influence everyone's way of thinking. Your mess may be the message for one person, and that is okay.

Surround yourself with those who challenge, empower, and hold you accountable but overall love you. The best way to apply this concept to your life is to analyze and determine who you are not, as I mentioned in an earlier chapter. Ask yourself, what am I not okay with? What works for my life, my world, and in my Matrix? If I die today or tomorrow how will my focus, my energy, and my attention be described? Was it worth it? Was it conducive to my destiny and my purpose?

It's normal to warn our brain and heart of these moments when our intuition is hinting at us, but are we truly prepared to live the reality of it? I made it clear that I was removing from my path those who are silent, complacent, voluntarily blind or ignorant to the fuckery. There are no exceptions to that requirement for me. The existing appreciation and love I held for the support showed to me as a teen mom and young wife navigating the ups and downs of a failing marriage and more will never be reduced nor will it be outweighed by estrangement. I consciously remind myself, "We are busting generational fuckery and anyone not on that wave is a part of the problem."

The hardest part is waking up and living out your decision everyday. Jaime Lima's words from the podcast where she talked about others losing sight of your value is a reminder. My decisions were called "childish", and I was accused of "once again being emotional". Yet this was a thoughtful, calculated, vented and vetted decision. Ed Mylett encourages you to identify your emotional house – the emotion you tend to go to. Over the last few years I have become very aware of my surroundings, my energy, and my response. I have managed to think things through, sleep or vent to those who do not consider me emotionally unstable. As I have said before, it was a necessity.

I am proud of myself for thinking differently. I no longer had to compromise, make adjustments, or be silent. I get to be me. Completely me, unapologetic. Healing out loud. Turning my pain into power and being an example, a sign that it is possible. It is painfully possible to make choices that serve you. It is painfully possible to grow into the person you are supposed to be, surrounded by the people who truly see you. Those who are meant to be there.

This is a story of a girl who made a decision to sever ties with family in order to reflect on fuckery and generational mentalities that cause discrepancies in the world she wanted for herself. In a world where everyone is breaking generational curses, it is one thing to say it and another to live it. A girl who leaned on unfamiliar resources to heal from trauma. Music, podcasts, books, spirituality and amazing humans whom she allowed in her world helped ease the pain of the decision to no longer partake in the fuckery and begin the road of healing. I decided to (in the words of Mel Robbins), "Let them." I will be silenced no more, my pain became my power as I continued this path of healing of loud.

"I don't get bitter, I just get better" - Erica Mason

I want to share this last thought with you in hopes that it will help you too. Throughout the journey of preparing to release this book I have found strength. I have questioned whether I should even release the words in this book because I didn't know what to expect. I've continued to consider those I called family, or the backlash of the mentality that I should respect my family and be grateful I have parents at all.

Yet the collective experience of reopening the lines of communication with my parents has reaffirmed for me that I can be an example of how hard this decision can be. Healing out loud because silence doesn't heal. This isn't about my parents or me. It's about those who believe no one will understand them because they have always felt different. How much exposure to your awesomeness is too much? How much do you include them in your life? How much do you share? How vulnerable will you allow yourself to be? Are they capable of being a contributing factor in your life? When will conversations get awkward? When will you be reminded of the fuckery? Do you have to rent a rug to sweep things under during your interactions because certain topics are still off the table?

These are all questions and realities I've had to face as I learn my new boundaries. Some shared moments have been great, like inviting them to join us for Mother's Day brunch at the amazing Thayer Hotel in West Point NY or coordinating their 30th wedding anniversary dinner. Likewise, there have been moments of disgust too. I share this part because allowing people back in or involving yourself again can continue to suck when conversations that are necessary are not had.

After one interaction in particular, I recalled an exchange of words and my chest got tight and my stomach was heavy. I finally understood. This will be a long road. I cried hard that night. I cry for the young girl inside of me. I continue to mourn the relationship I wish I had with my parents and thought I had with my brother. I feel for others going through this too. I share this to give you, as the person hoping the fuckery would stop, some insight that it is a continuous process. Their lives don't stop because you're not a part of it. It's the Let Them Theory in full swing. Thank you, Mel Robbins! It's replacing years of life with these humans, it's having precious memories shadowed by nauseating realities. I've made several strides in my healing. I credit music, podcasts and all of those who have stayed in my life or entered my life in the last eight years. The ones who have truly supported and seen me. And we need that!

The painful truth in growth and healing is that it's a continuum of reducing expectations. It's a learning process that may feel silly at times because with billions of people on this planet we are worried about a handful of them. That's because you loved them so much once and you would never treat others that way.

Although I am not 100% sure where this will lead, I will continue my journey of healing out loud and encouraging others to do the same. Be a renegade like Eminem and live your truth like Erica Mason. Let Them like Mel Robbins. Know that "your breaking point is God's building point" like Ed Mylett said. You're not different, you're the first one. The first to say, "This ends with me." So, my friend, let this book and my story inspire you to continue to Heal Out Loud.

"The best way to add meaning to an experience is to look for how it may serve you in the future"
- Jay Shetty, Think Like A Monk

Acknowledgement

First and foremost, God has gotten me here, and I am grateful! My ancestors, angels, and the universe have guided and protected me. May I continue to make choices that fulfill His purpose for my life.

To my husband, thank you for being my battery pack and soundboard. I'm so proud of us.

To my firstborn, you have seen me through it all. Thank you for being patient with me as I grow up.

To my second and third born, you both challenge me to be patient and self-aware. Thank you for facilitating my growth.

To all the strong women in my life, thank you for loving me unconditionally through this.

I will be forever grateful for the divine timing of meeting my writing coach, Giselle. Your prayers, patience, and support have facilitated my growth and healing, and I love you for it. Thank you for helping me execute this journey of helping others find theirs.

www.ingramcontent.com/pod-product-compliance
Lightning Source LLC
Chambersburg PA
CBHW060405090426
42734CB00011B/2264